The Uninvited Guest

The Uninvited Guest

Histories of Persian theatre in the Qajar Period

Duman Riyazi

ASEMANA BOOKS

Toronto, Canada
FIRST EDITION

Published by ASEMANA BOOKS

ISBN: 9781997503354

Book Design: Asemana Books

Cover Art: Asemana Books

To find out more about our authors and books visit: www.asemanabooks.ca

ASEMANA BOOKS

Contents

Acknowledgements and Author's Note

This book is the result of a journey that extended far beyond archives, libraries, and historical documents. It is the outcome of years spent searching, travelling, and retracing the routes once taken by Naser al-Din Shah Qajar and Mozaffar al-Din Shah Qajar across Europe and beyond.

In pursuit of this story, I travelled from city to city and country to country, standing in railway stations, theatres, museums, palaces, streets, and archives where fragments of this forgotten history still lingered. Many answers proved elusive, many doors remained closed, and many discoveries emerged only through years of patience, uncertainty, exhaustion, and persistence.

What now appears in these pages is the product of countless hours of travel, research, translation, comparison, interpretation, and reflection, a long and demanding journey sustained by a belief in the value of recovering overlooked histories and forgotten encounters.

Above all, I wish to express my deepest gratitude to Professor Siro Ferrone. Throughout the years of research that carried me from one archive to another and from one city to the next, his friendship, encouragement, and unwavering support remained a constant source of strength. Many of the challenges encountered during this scholarly journey would have been far more difficult to overcome without his trust and generosity.

I am also indebted to the archivists, librarians, curators, researchers, and custodians of historical collections whose dedication to preserving the documentary record makes work such as this possible. If part of this forgotten story can be told once again today, it is thanks in no small measure to those who have safeguarded the traces of the past.

A Note on Documents and Illustrations

In a limited number of cases, readers will encounter descriptions of historical documents rather than reproductions of the original materials themselves. This decision was not made for scholarly reasons but was necessitated by restrictions related to publication and reproduction rights.

Many of the documents consulted for this book were obtained from archives, libraries, and collections across several countries. Although copies of the original materials are in the author's possession, some institutions required reproduction fees for publication that exceeded the financial capacity of this independently funded project.

Because every stage of this research, from archival travel and document acquisition to translation, analysis, and writing, was undertaken independently and at personal expense, without institutional sponsorship or external funding, it was occasionally necessary to provide detailed descriptions of certain documents in place of reproducing the originals.

It is my hope that this decision will not diminish the reader's engagement with the material or the historical significance of the sources themselves, which remain central to many of the arguments and findings presented throughout this volume.

Finally, I would like to thank you, the reader. Historical research often begins with a single question and ends with many more. If this book encourages a deeper reflection on the cultural encounters, performances, misunderstandings, and exchanges that shaped relations between Iran and Europe in the nineteenth century, then the years devoted to this undertaking will have been well spent.

Duman Riyazi
Toronto, Canada
2026

CHAPTER 1:

A HISTORY OF PERSIAN THEATRE

As history confirms, monotheistic religions generally have fewer theatrical displays than polytheistic ones. In Persia, two religions alternated (and are still present together): Islam and Zoroastrianism. This was often the cause of internal wars; and probably for this reason there were not many different kinds of entertainment in Persia.[1] The shows originally came from the religious customs of the primitive tribes, and even later, when they separated from them, they still depended on the latter. The religious leaders even accepted the performances and used them as a means of promoting the religion itself.[2]

1. Before Islam

About two thousand years before Christ, a group of Indo-Europeans arrived and settled in Persia. Subsequently, other tribes of different ethnicities arrived, which led to numerous wars. Only after the wars ended, when the new culture began to take into account the language, habits and traditions of diverse local populations.[3] could cultural integration be observed. In primitive society, it was common to hunt and eat together, and every evening the chief regaled all the members of the tribe with stories about the hunt or the war. This form of storytelling, which was characterized by emphasized or ezaggerated body language,[4] was designed as

[1] Bahram Beyzaee, *Theatre in Iran*, [Namāyish dar Īrān], Roshangaran, Tehran 1964, 2.

[2] Ibid

[3] Ibid 18.

[4] Ibid 2.

the first form of Persian theatrical performance and was called naghali.[5] The performers who orally transmitted the primitive stories added episodes about the protagonists' war deeds and hunts, so that this type of performance grew over time from one generation to the next and was enriched with imaginative interludes.[6] In their implementation, the tribal chiefs envisaged a circular arrangement of the audience around the narrator, following the model of the first theatrical events. The people also saw the performance as a form of entertainment, and this contributed significantly to the growth in importance of the theater.[7]

The addition of primitive masks, which made the story more realistic, also meant an advance in artistic elaboration. A document from this period that proves the aforementioned is the book of the Persian historian Abobakr Mohammad ebn Jafar al Narshakhi (899-959). In 943, he reported in the *Tarikhe Narshekhi*[8] how the people of Bukhara[9] wept and prayed for Siavash,[10] who was killed by the hand of Afrasiab,[11] recalling that this tradition goes back about three thousand years. In Penjkent[12] (Tajikistan) there is a painting depicting the ceremony associated with this tradition. Ctesias of Cnidus and Herodotus then report a ceremony in 522 BC called Megaphonia. This festival was a kind of ceremonial spectacle from the Akmenid period, in which the story was

[5] See in the same chapter of this work

[6] Bahram Beyzaee, *Theatre in Iran*, [Namāyish dar Īrān], cit., pp. 60-61

[7] Yaghub Azhand, *theatre of the Safavids*, [Namāyish dar dawrah-ʾi Ṣafavī],Asare Honari, Tehran 2009, pp. 200-203

[8] Abubakr Narshakhi, *The history of Bukhara*, Tus, Tehran 2008, pp. 38-21.

[9] Bukhara is a city in Uzbekistan which, at the end of the reign of Nadir Shah (1736-1747) was part of Persia.

[10] Mythological character who appears in the manuscript entitled Shah Name of Firdusi. Siavash was the son of Kay Kāvus, the king of the Kayanian dynasty.

[11] This mythical king and hero of Turan is the main antagonist of the Persian epic Shahnameh written by Ferdowsi.

[12] City in Suğd Region, Tajikistan.

Fig. 1. The Penjikent fresco (in Tajikistan) illustrates the ritual crying ceremony of the people of Bukhara for Siavash, From Archaeology in the USSR, Gustav Glaesser, Istituto Italiano per l'Africa e l'Oriente (IsIAO).

performed of a priest who had begun to rule by deceit after the murder of the king's brother. When the members of the court realized his true identity, they killed him. This festival was thus marked by the remembrance of historical and political events to warn the population.[13] There was also another prayer custom that relied on scenic dialogue in its development: the use of the Avesta[14] book, as typical of the Zoroastrians. We know that there were dialogues in some parts of the Gat, but we are not sure if they can really be considered as a kind of prelude or precursor of the theatre.[15] However, other spectacular customs from this period are still present today. As Bahram Beyzaee suggests, there are documents that testify that the Persians killed Marcus Licinius Crassus[16] in 53 BC during the war between Persia and Rome led by the famous captain Surena. At the end of the war, Persian soldiers found a Roman soldier very similar

[13] John M. Marincola, *the Histories*, (London, Penguiin, 1959), 209.

[14] Holy book of the Zoroastrian religion.

[15] Bahram Beyzaee, *Theatre in Iran*, [Namāyish dar Īrān], 21.

[16] Surena (84 BC - 52 BC) belonged to one of the most important families of the Parthian Empire (247 BC - 224 AD). Marcus Licinius Crassus (115 BC -53 BC) was a politician and military commander of the Republic Roman.

to Crassus; they forced him to wear women's clothes and paraded him through the city to humiliate the enemy. This spectacular form was later reproduced before the king.[17]

Another spectacular symbolic tradition was the Kuse bar neshin[18] celebrated in December. On one day of the month, probably from November 20 to December 10, a beardless man was chosen in most Persian cities to mount a donkey holding a crow in his right hand and a fan in his left.[19] It is likely that in this ancient custom that the crow symbolized winter and the ritual as a whole the transition from spring (March-November) to winter (November-March). This tradition continued after the advent of Islam and was given another name: Mir Noroozi.[20] The Persian calendar indicated

---

[17] Bahram Beyzaee, *Theatre in Iran*, [Namāyish dar Īrān], 29-30.

[18] In ancient Persia, people believed that the earth was born in spring and grew in summer, and that it began to age in autumn and died in winter. To call the earth to its rebirth, shows were held, so as to welcome spring.
On the first day of winter the people in most of Persia, especially in the North, would choose an old, beardless man and a donkey. The old man mounted the donkey with a crow in one hand and a fan in the other hand, and went out of the city, with his face made up with spices. People threw stones at him to get him away.
We still don't know why the old man took a crow, we can interpret that the gesture wanted to show the end of winter and the arrival of spring.
Abo Reyhan Biruni's book Al Tafhim ol explains: "In the month of Azar a man sat on a donkey, with a crow in one hand and a fan in the other with which he greeted winter."
Instead Emad ol Din Zakariya Gazvini in the book entitled Ajaeb ol Makhlughat and Garaeb ol Mojudat says: «On the first day of the month of Azar called Hormoz a beardless man, sitting on the donkey wore his old clothes. People gave him hot sweets, with a face made up with warm colors and spices, in one hand a fan, and in the other a crow, always saying: «he It's hot, it's hot. People laughed at him and threw trash at him."

[19] Abu Rayhan Muhammad ibn Ahmad al-*Biruni, Al Tafhim,*(Tehran Majles, 1937), 256-257.

[20] The ancient Persian calendar had twelve months of thirty days and the last five days of the year were the special ones of the remembered stolen palm. As the great Persian philosopher Al-Biruni says in Asar ol Bagieh

Fig: 2 An example for Kuse Bar neshin, Archive of Golestan Place, Qajar period.

several important events that required festivals, from which primitive spectacular forms emerged. In ancient Persia, each year had two seasons and twelve months, and each month had thirty days. Thus, in a Persian year, the 365 days of the solar always lacked five, which were called the "stolen palm.[21]" During these five days, the population devoted

(The remaining signs of past centuries): «The fifteenth day of the month of Gods is called Dibmehr, people built a doll that resembled that beardless old man, of whom we have explained, they paid him many respects and, in the end, they burned it». After the affirmation of Islam this custom also developed in Egypt, where it was proposed on the first day of spring, which was the Norooz festival. On the day of the Mir Noroozi festival people would choose a beardless man, make him up with flour and put on a yellow or red suit. Then the chosen one was made to get on a mule to take a tour of the city. Proceeding in this way, the Mir asked those present for money; if he didn't receive them and his companions threw dirty water on people.

The nobles, during the party, stayed at home, while the poor stayed outside the house, along the street. If a nobleman left his home they threw the water at him, unless he paid enough to witness the scene. The students went to school and started beating the teachers. If the teachers paid, however, they could save themselves from beatings.

[21] Abu Rayhan Muhammad ibn Ahmad al-Biruni, translated by Akbar, Danaseresht, *Asar ol bagieh*,(Tehran Amir Kabir, 1984), 68-69.

themselves to charitable activities such as painting, renovating and cleaning the municipal buildings or organizing events. Among the peculiarities of Persian traditions was also the celebration of special dates marked by the names of the days and months. For example, since both the fourth month of the Persian calendar and the thirteenth day of each month are called Tir,[22] Persians celebrated great festivals on the thirteenth day of the month of Tir.[23] Nezami Ganjavi, the greatest Persian epic poet (1141-1209), reports in his poem *Haft peykar*[24] that in the Sassanid period in Persia there was a king named Bahram Gur (421-438). At that time, the government allowed six thousand actors from India to stay in the country to show new spectacular and theatrical forms.[25] However, there are no documents from the period before Islam to prove this, and if there were any, they have been lost. It is almost impossible to find material from this period, because it must be remembered that theatrical performances in Persia were essentially popular and that there was no one to write the texts or report on the performances at that time: if there were performances, they were entirely improvised.[26]

2. *After Islam*

Islam is a religion whose motto is equality and brotherhood. This new creed did not know much about art and entertainment, for reasons I will not enumerate here.[27] Characteristic of the society of that time was the affirmation of rituals, customs and performances that corresponded to

---

22 It is the fourth month of the Solar Hijri calendar, which is the official calendar of Persia.

23 Hashem Razi, *The calendar of ancient Persia*, Pizhūhishī dar gāhshumārī va jashn'hā-yi Īrān-i bāstān(Tehran Farvehar, 1979), 68

24 Nezami, *Haft Peykar*,Ebn sina, Tehran 1955.

25 Ibid 106.

26 Bahram, Beyzaee, *Theatre in Iran*, [Namāyish dar Īrān], 41.

27 Ibid 44.

the Islamic religion. If some traditional customs were not well regarded, they were abandoned; on the contrary, if they were considered virtuous (always based on the criteria of the religion), they were encouraged.[28] Until today, some terms referring to performances before the Islamic period have remained in use. One of them is *tamasha* or "spectacle," a word that in its most general meaning is used today in Persian to refer to any form of performance.[29] Two types of spectacle traditions have survived to this day (Kuse bar neshin and the Megafonia festival, which we have already discussed), although it must be said that even as these realities have preserved their original structure, with the advent of Islam they took on other names and underwent slight changes in terms of their construction. The protagonists of these forms that we have been talking about were figures destined to become famous and who aroused great interest among the population.[30] Later, in the Qajar period,[31] these characters gave rise to an important form of Persian theatrical performance called Takhteh hozi. These characters are mainly three: Haji firooz, the main mask of Persian comedy in the form of a black-skinned man with red clothes, a drum and a red hat; Atash afruz, the firemen; Ghul biabuni[32], an Orc. Characteristic of traditional Persian tamasha are mainly sleight of hand, acrobatics and magic tricks. With the spread of religion to all levels of society, the Islamic component was also incorporated into the artistic sphere. Thus, a new type of religious show gradually spread: the ta'ziyah.[33] We briefly present some spectacular forms, which we will discuss in more detail in the following chapters.

---

[28] Ibid 44-45

[29] Ibid 45.

[30] Bahram Beyzaee, *Theatre in Iran*, [Namāyish dar Īrān], 46.

[31] From 1794 to 1925.

[32] Bahram Beyzaee, *Theatre in Iran*, [Namāyish dar Īrān], 48.

[33] Ibid 49.

Naghali

The Naghali was a type of ancient Persian show in which a person told a story with mythological, religious, and heroic themes using body movements and expressive voice modulation. This spectacular form also dates back to the time before the affirmation of Islam in Persia, when it took the name Ghavali.[34] A person told a story accompanied by a musical instrument (perhaps a harp). The actors who participated were called Ravi.[35] The great Persian writer Bahram Beyzaee writes in his book on spectacle in Iran that there were various forms of Naghali.[36]

Fig.3. An example for Naghali, Archive of Golestan Place, Qajar period.

1) Shahnameh Khani

Several people narrated the episodes of a book of epic poetry, *Shahnameh* (The Book of Kings), written by a great poet (Ferdowsi) who lived in the tenth century.

---

[34] Ibid

[35] It means narrator, but in this text it is a type of actor who plays and sings

[36] Bahram Beyzaee, *Theatre in Iran*, [Namāyish dar Īrān], 72-76.

2) Hamleh Khani

An actor recited part of Hamleye Heydari,[37] which depicts the wars of Ali, a saint of Islam and successor of Muhammad.

3) Rozeh Khani

Two actors narrated the story of the city of Karbala[38] or a story about the lives and passions of Islamic saints. In the scene, the actors exaggerated the movements of the body and made the audience cry, also thanks to the repeated hitting on the head as a sign of repentance, invoking the name of the saint whose deeds they represented.

Fig.4. An example for Rozeh Khani, Archive of Golestan Place, Qajar period

4) Pardeh Khani

Another type of Persian storytelling spectacle that, in addition to the presence of an actor, required a tent

[37] The text was taken from a lyric poem by the writer Bazel Mashhadi (11th century) which narrates various stories of Mohammed and Ali.
[38] City of Iraq and second holy city for Muslims

on which to see drawings inspired by the events of various religious and mythological stories, and sometimes by love. The interpreter told the story with the help of body movements and changing voice tones, holding a stick called Metragh with which he pointed at figures painted on the tent to facilitate the narration.

The puppet play

In Iran there were two main types of puppetry:[39]

- Kheymeh shab bazi (puppet play);

- Sayeh bazi (shadow play).

The main characters of this form of play were five:[40]
1) Pahlevan kachal (the bald master);
2) Akhond;[41]
3) Bibi (an old woman);
4) Rostam (a very strong man, like Hercules);
5) The fiend.

Other characters could be added if needed. The actor who operated the puppets was called Ostad[42] or Master. He was always assisted by an assistant who helped him sing and make the puppets speak. For this purpose, a small wind instrument (called a *safir*[43]) was used, which was placed behind the lower teeth.

There were also two people who accompanied the show with musical instruments: the Kamancheh and the Tonbak. One

---

[39] Bahram Beyzaee, *Theatre in Iran*, [Namāyish dar Īrān], 82
[40] Ibid 100.
[41] The mullah
[42] Bahram Beyzaee, *Theatre in Iran*, [Namāyish dar Īrān], 106.
[43] Whistle.

of these two musicians, called Morshed,[44] also played the role of narrator, providing the audience with the necessary information to understand the nature of the environment evoked by the scenario and the roles of the characters. The Ostad and the Morshed were also the ones who took care of the organization of the performance: narration, development, etc. This form of performance was also known in Persia by other names that are still used today, including:[45]

1) ***Khial bazi (dream play):*** characterized by episodes that can be considered real only in dreams.

2) ***Shab bazi (play of the night):*** a form of play that was always performed in a dark place.

3) ***Pardeh bazi (screen play):*** so called because the spectators saw only the shadows reflected on a screen.

4) ***Lobat bazi (Puppet play):*** a play characterized by the presence of puppets.

5) ***Sorat baz or Lobat[46] baz:*** sorat means "face," Baz was a suffix that referred to the actor who performed this type of play, while Lobat was the puppet used for the play.

Ta'ziyah

The Ta'ziyah is a religious drama that tells various stories about Islamic saints and especially about the history of the city of Karbala.[47] Some Persian theorists believe that this

---

[44] Bahram Beyzaee, *Theatre in Iran*, [Namāyish dar Īrān], 106.

[45] Ibid 103.

[46]The term can mean toy or lover, and can refer to a good-looking person or thing. Mohammad Moein, *Persian Dictionary*, Farhang-i Fārsī, (TehranAmir Kabir, 1971), 892.

[47] Bahram Beyzaee, *Theatre in Iran*, [Namāyish dar Īrān], 116.

spectacular form originated from ancient Persian myths such as Siavash.[48]
Persian history has confirmed that a government that wants to rule rigidly and directly needs the religious instrument and the consent of the people. Seeing that the Sunni Ottomans had created a very strong and compact empire, the Safavids began to declare themselves Shiites in order to be able to simultaneously fight the Turks and define their own, albeit Islamic, identity.[49] As a result, a strong unity based on culture and identity emerged in Persia: this also affected the Ta'ziyah, which was greatly affected by the religious dictates of the Safavid government.[50] Given the enormous popularity that Ta'ziyah received, the Safavid government began building theaters to promote this type of performance and also to patronize religious poets.

Fig. 5. Ta'ziyah in Qajar Period, Archive of Golestan Place, Qajar period.

[48] Mohammad amin Kalateh, *The oldest religious mourning*, «Newspaper of Tehran emruz», 1.12.2011.
[49] William Bayne Fisher, translator Yaghub Azhand, *History of the Safavids*, (Tehran Jami, 1949), 27-28.
[50] Yaghub Azhand, *theatr of the Safavids*, [Namāyish dar dawrah-'i Ṣafavī] ,39.

If we wanted to explain the evolution of the Ta'ziyah until it reached its final form, we could say that its historical narrative went through the following phass of actualization:[51]

1) Groups of prisoners passed in a procession consisting of two long lines in front of the people who had gathered to watch the event. All the figures clapped their hands on their chests and struck each other on the shoulders with chains. There were also figures carrying large religious symbols similar to instruments of war. Still others played musical instruments such as cymbals and drums. One person sang or illustrated the story of Karbala or other religious incidents while the people watched in chorus.

2) Later, two or three actors dressed as saints were added to replace those who originally sang to describe the story of the city of Karbala.

3) In a third moment, dialogs were introduced between the different actors.

The French traveler and merchant Jean-Baptiste Tavernier[52] claims in his book *Les six voyages* that he saw a five-hour performance of Ta'ziyah.[53] Women were not allowed to play any role in the plays: the female roles were played by men in disguise. As in all theater genres, there is the positive component as opposed to the negative, the protagonist versus the antagonist. The saints and their families were clearly the positive elements, and they always wore white or green clothes that allowed their roles to be recognized without the possibility of ambiguity. The enemies, on the

[51] Yaghub Azhand, *Theatre of the Qajars*, (Namāyish dar dawrah-i Qājār), cit., pp 142-147.
[52] French traveler born in Paris in 1605.
[53] Jean-Baptiste Tavernier, translator Hamid Arbab Shiran, *Les Six voy*ages,(Tehran Nilufar, 2002), 414

other hand, always wore red.[54] Aleksander Borejko Chodźko (1804-1891), Polish politician and orientalist, claimed in his work on Iranian theatre that a person was said to have found thirty-three texts of ta'ziyah.[55] There are two different types of ta'ziyah:[56]

1) The Ta'ziyah mozhek (Ridiculous Ta'ziyah), in which actors joke with their colleagues playing the role of enemies and provoke them by exaggerating in dialogues and stage movements.

2) The ta'ziyah zanane (ta'ziyah for women only), which is performed by women only. This type of theater took place in the houses and gardens of aristocrats.

Takhteh Hozi

The term Takhteh Hozi is composed of two words meaning "wood" and "well." In ancient Persia, it was customary for this form of spectacle to place wooden platforms on top of a well, which was located in most courtyards of houses.[57]

The audience was then arranged around the well while the actors performed on the platform. After the advent of Islam (633 AD), society changed so much that comedies and shows were also affected by this change.

There was a tendency to stage more and more satirical works about the Muslim reality in Persia; however, what was supposed to make people laugh only provoked ridicule due to

---

[54] Yaghub Azhand, *Theatre of the Qajars*,(Namāyish dar dawrah-i Qājār),102-103

[55]Aleksandro Chodzko, translator Jalal Satari, The Iranian Theater, (Tehran Faslnameye Theatre), 1990.

[56] Bahram Beyzaee, *Theatre in Iran*, [Namāyish dar Īrān], 160-161.

[57] Yaghub Azhand, *Theatre of the Qajars*, (Namāyish dar dawrah-i Qājār), 278.

the sad reality of the time.[58] In such a context, one can notice a strong censorship by the government, even at the level of theater: all performances were allowed to speak only about certain topics and in certain ways, so as not to cause problems with the authorities.

The radical change in Persian society also affected the ancient tamasha, which was performed by itinerant actors after the arrival of Islam With the end of the Safavid period, the history of Persian entertainment comes to an important point in its history. From this point on, the term Tamasha is no longer used to define any kind of show: each individual type is given its own name. In the last years of this era, caravans of actors moved from town to town, with horses and suitcases loaded with instruments for the plays and with all the props. These traveling troupes were invited by famous or wealthy families.[59] There were also two other types of performances that were highly appreciated by the people: (Taghlid-Mazhake),[60] in which the final scene was always characterized by a violent feigned quarrel between the actors,[61] who were called luti, which had great physical force.[62]

There were three interpreters who impersonated members of different social classes and spoke with the different accents and inflections of their respective social classes.[63] The actors had to adapt to the language of the social class in which they were performing. In the late Safavid period, lutis often performed in coffee houses and were invited by people of different backgrounds to entertain wedding guests.[64]

---

58 Bahram Beyzaee, *Theatre in Iran*, [Namāyish dar Īrān], 166-167.

59 Ibid 169.

60 See in the second chapter of this work.

61 Yaghub Azhand, *Theatre of the Qajars*, (Namāyish dar dawrah-i Qājār)], 220-221.

62 Ibid 214.

63 Bahram Beyzaee, *Theatre in Iran*, [Namāyish dar Īrān], 168-169.

64 Ibid 169.

We have already said that there were chests in which the actors placed show instruments: it often happened that the actors themselves came out of the chests. In fact, the performance began with supporting actors who brought these chests on stage, from which, as soon as the music started, the actors hidden inside came out and began the play.[65]

Different types of performances enriched the versatility of the Takhteh hozi. Especially important was the kachalak bazi (literally, "play of a bald man"): in this play, a bald, unemployed idler in love with a beautiful or rich girl goes to her house to ask for her hand in marriage, but the girl's father does not accept.[66] In Takhteh hozi, as in Commedia dell'Arte, there are two main characters, namely the servants and the old men.[67] The most important character is undoubtedly Siah, a dark-skinned man with red clothes, a drum and a red hat, very intelligent and with the body of a gymnast.

He eats a lot and works little, always sings and dances and often jokes with people, especially with his boss and superior, Arbab (Haji Posh), the main character among those who make up the group of old men.

We will follow the development of the Takhte hozi in the Safavid and Qajar periods (1587-1925), which was particularly important for the development of all traditional Persian theater forms. Another very interesting type of performance was the Baghal bazi. The story is about a stupid and stingy owner of a grocery store who has in his employ a bumbling servant who makes mistakes in every action. In addition, there are two sly customers who want to steal something from him, and all four speak with a special accent: the jokes in this situation became more and more ridiculous.

---

[65] Ibid.

[66] Ibid 51.

[67] Yaghub Azhand, *Theatre of the Qajars*,(Namāyish dar dawrah-i Qājār), 282.

In the period of the Zand[68] dynasty, individual actors gradually joined groups, which already consisted of several actors, and formed new theater groups.[69]

[68] The Zand dynasty ruled central and southern Iran in the second half of the 18th century.
[69] Bahram Beyzaee, *Theatre in Iran*, [Namāyish dar Īrān], 168-172.

CHAPTER 2:

THEATRE IN PERSIA'S QAJAR PERIOD

As mentioned above, "Naghali" was one of the most important and popular plays of the Qajar period. Oral literature and historical fiction can take spectacular forms. In fact, oral literature has been one of the most important forms of expression in Persia since ancient times. This spectacular form also dates back to Islam and has received the official name of Ghavali in modern times. In it, a person told a story accompanied by a musical instrument, perhaps a harp. The actors who told the story were called ravi.

In this play, the first actor is the Naghal. The Naghali renders the story of a fable (mythological, religious, heroic) or a poem, with special body movements and language games performed before the audience. Naghali can also take other forms: Shahname Khani, Hamle Khani, Roze Khani, Parde Khani.

In the Qajar period, there were two specific types of Naghali: those who worked among the people and in the markets were professionals who were first-rate at their job; other Naghali, who usually worked in the courts for the princes or nobles, changed the story according to the wishes of their patrons.

Malcolm writes in the second volume of his book *History of Persia* that in the local court of the Qajars there were always actors who told stories from the famous books of ancient Persia. Their stories were extremely humuorous, and especially when the king was tired, they made him relax. The narrator always tried to soften the harsher rough parts.[70]

---

[70] John Malcolm, translator Mirza Ismail Heyrat, *History of Persia*, Afsun 1990, 552.

Benning,[71] the Scottish traveler, in his book *A Journal of Two Years' Travel in Persia,*[72] notes an excellent point about a Naghali performance in which the Naghal tells the story of Koroghlu's life in the Azeri language with his musical instruments. From his story and description we can surmise the performer to have been an Ashik.[73]

In the Qajar period, the Naghali retained an extremely causal relationship with the places where it was performed. One place where the academic Naghali performance usually took place was the Ghahve Khaneh. In the Safavid period, actors usually performed in squares and markets or sometimes in cafes, but during the Qajar era the Ghahve khaneh became the main performance venue for this play. However, this local change started in Isfahan and then was transferred to other cities such as Shiraz and Tabriz.

In the major cities of Iran, the Naghali regularly had a special time for their performances, such as the month of Ramadan or the New Year or other religious holidays. Some naghali, in order to earn money, traveled between cities in Iran and performed in ghahve khane and other public places during their travel. Among them were people who traveled to cities as far away as Mecca.

The play didn't take place during the day when people were working. Each naghal performed his show in two or three ghahve khane and was able to earn money for his day-to-day expenses.

In the last years of Safavid rule, other types of naghali began to be established, such as the Shamayel gardani or the Parde dari: a type of religious naghali held in front of a tent

---

[71] Binning, Robert B.M.(1814-1891).

[72]Robert B. M. Binning, *A Journal of Two Years' Travel in Persia*, 2 vols, (London, Ceylon, 1857).

[73] Traditional form of Azeri Musical Performance. The performer (Ashik), narrate and plays the special musical instrument (Saz), the one of the folklore story of Azerbaijan.

designed with stories on a religious theme in which Islamic saints were the main characters. The integration of images and narratives formed the unfolding of the play. As the actor began the narration by pointing to the images on the curtain, he demonstrated the techniques of Naghali. He explained the whole story with his body movements and voice. As soon as he got to a point where the story became critically significant, he would stop and interrogate people for money. At that time he continued the narration to the end.

In the Qajar period, Parde Khani flourished on a large scale, and Persian painters adopted new drawing styles from abroad. Many of these styles were influenced by the Ghahve Khane technique and drew inspiration from the history of saints and religious forms.

The Parde Khani play was unusual for the people of the countryside, where it was difficult to organize the Ta'ziyah. However, for the Parde Khani, there was no need for a large-scale organization. This, therefore, made it possible to bring the theater to peripheral regions as well.

In the Qajar period, when coffee houses became the main venue for the presentation of Naghali and Parde Khani, many coffee house owners invited painters to create the tents required for the performances.

Usually, the master paid the artists, provided them with lodgings, and signed their paintings at the end. From the information we have about the tents, we can say that they had two distinct and significant themes: religious history and mythology. It was rare to find paintings inspired by ancient history or love stories on the tent.

Anyway, Naqali, one of the earliest Iranian theatrical forms, emerged during the Qajar period despite the religious and political challenges it faced and eventually evolved into a more refined and established art form.

2. The religious form of play: the Ta'ziyah .

According to the dictionary of the authoritative Iranian linguist Allameh Ali Akbar Dehkhoda, "Ta'ziyah is nothing but the creative form for funeral rites. In this case, it is often used for the commemoration of Ali and Husayn.[74]" According to another well-known vocabulary edited by Hasan Amid, Rozeh Khani is a ritual performed primarily in honor of Islamic saints or Imams.[75]

This play depicts the events of Kerbelā, a village in southern Mesopotamia, where on October 10, 680, al-Ḥusayn ibn Ali, the nephew of the Prophet Muhammad and the son of the fourth caliph Ali ibn, was killed along with his family, his entourage Abī Ṭālib, and Muhammad's daughter, Fāṭima al-Zahrā. The causes of the Kerbelā massacre, carried out by the Umayyad troops of the Walidi Kufa ʿUbayd Allāh ibn Ziyād, faithful to the caliph Yazīd ibn Muʿāwiya ibn Abī Sufyān, are rooted in the struggle between the Alide family (which considered itself the only one entitled to govern the Umma) and the descendants of Muʿāwiya ibn Abī Sufyān, the founder of the caliphal dynasty of Damascus. After the events of Siffīn and the arbitration of Adhruḥ, there was an imminent assassination of the caliph Ali by the Kharijite Ibn Muljam. Following this, there was a short-lived attempt by the eldest son of the deceased caliph, al-Hasan ibn Ali, but the candidacy of Mu'awiya allowed no more opponents upon his ascent to the Islamic judiciary.[76]

During the Safavid period, Ta'ziyah was not regarded as a specific spectacular form, but rather as different art forms that were predominantly "separate" from each other. From

---

[74] Ali Akbar Dehkhoda, *Dehkhoda Dictionary*, Lughatnāmah-'i Fārsī Banke, (Tehran Melli, 1940), 330.

[75] Hasan Amid, *Amid vocabulary*, Farhang-i 'Amīd (Fārsī), (Tehran, Amir kabir, 1983), 554.

[76] Bahram Beyzai, *Theatre in Iran*, [Namāyish dar Īrān], 116.117.

the ultimate end of this period, on the contrary, a process began whereby all the alternative theatrical forms merged into a single new form which took the name of Ta'ziyah.[77]

In the reign of Shah Sultan Husayn,[78] the previous ruler of the Safavid dynasty, it is possible to begin to notice the presence of some typical characteristics of Ta'ziyah which increasingly take on the form that will be definitive later on.

For example, in the Ta'ziyah, which primarily focuses on the events of Karbala, it is evident that the depiction of historical events in a purely theatrical manner is becoming more prominent, thus establishing itself as a characteristic feature of this type of play.

Another feature that began to establish itself is the presence of a sarcophagus carried on two bars, symbolizing the funerary component typical of this show. It must be said that those who took part in this demonstration began to have the awareness that they were not simple or casual extras, but rather real actors following a precise ritual.

The Ta'ziyah evolves and reaches its absolute form in four historical periods:[79]

• The reign of Fath Ali Shah;

• The reign of Mohammad Shah;

• The reign of Naser Al-Din Shah;

• The reign of Mozaffar Al-Din Shah;

---

[77] Yaghub Azhand, *Theatre of the Qajars*,(Namāyish dar dawrah-i Qājār), 15.

[78] He was the last Safavid king of Persia and reigned from 1694 until his deposition by Mahmud Hotak, an ethnic Pashtun Afghan, in 1722.

[79] Yaghub Azhand, *Theatre of the Qajars*,(Namāyish dar dawrah-i Qājār), 15.

Each of these periods has its own peculiarities, but there is also a common denominator in the determined will of the rulers (all of whom belonged to the Qajar dynasty) to openly finance the show, to the extent that they almost became its patrons.

The Ta'ziyah during the reign of Fath Ali Shah (1772-1834)

It is important to note that the Qajar dynasty, which began with Agha Mohammad Khan, emerged during a politically turbulent period. There was a lack of national unity, and Persia's military weakness made it vulnerable to attacks from the Ottomans, Indians, and internal factions seeking autonomy. In such a delicate phase, theatre was naturally pushed into the background.

The ruler, Agha Mohammad Khan, was completely devoted to warfare. He was also an extremely religious individual. In fact, his only noteworthy act, culturally speaking, was the remodeling of Husayn's harem, where he used to spend a significant amount of time praying.

During this period the displays took place in houses, markets, courtyards, cemeteries, in the main squares of cities, or in caravanserais. Agha Mohammad Khan adopted a unique and controversial attitude. Despite being religious, he had, paradoxically, no contact with Islamic religious figures. When asked to organize a religious-theatrical event, such as Ta'ziyah, he remained indifferent, neither preventing nor encouraging it.

A significant and distinct change of gear took place with Fath Ali Shah. He succeeded his father and assumed a profile that encouraged and financed artistic and cultural forms, including the theater and the Ta'ziyah. He managed to capitalize on the fierce competition among the various theater companies by providing financial support to all of them and offering a significantly large cash prize to the company that staged the best show. This intense competition gave rise to highly sophisticated forms of musical entertainment. During this period, the displays took place in houses, markets, courtyards, cemeteries, and in the main squares of cities or caravanserais. Before the shows began, the Tekieh was built, which was a "mobile" structure (specifically, a tent) constructed for the occasion.

The greatness of the Tekieh depended on the significant contributions made by the sovereign and wealthy individuals in the area for the execution of the show. Generous funding resulted in the creation of a massive and magnificent tent, adorned with intricate and meticulously crafted details. Strictly speaking, however, a relatively modest Tekieh corresponded to limited funding.

In the Muslim world, charming women could not enthusiastically participate in the shows, which is why for the first time, during the reign of Fath Ali Shah, the Ta'ziyah for women only appeared, where they recited, played, and actively participated in every aspect of the play. It can be said that in a short time, there was an incredible "Ta'ziyah - effect"; this show typically involved more and more people to the point of spreading like an epidemic. Aristocrats, merchants, politicians, and everyone financed and encouraged this creative production.[80]

---

[80] Yaghub Azhand, *Theatre of the Qajars*, (Namāyish dar dawrah-i Qājār), 18.

The Ta'ziyah during the reign of Mohammad Shah (1834-1848)

During the years of the reign of Mohammad Shah, there were, at the political level, two treaties that damaged the Persian world; the treaty of Golestan[81] and that of Turkmenchay.[82] Furthermore, the strong English influence in neighboring India meant that the government of London, which had become the most powerful in the world, became involved in Persian affairs. This was done to ensure the protection of both the caravan routes and the English merchants who had to pass through Persia in order to reach India. The British had such a strong influence on the ruler of Tehran that if any Persian officials, even those in high positions, opposed concessions to the British, they would usually bring their complaints to the king. The king, without hesitation, would often confront (sometimes even physically) those who refused to acknowledge English rights in Persia.

This weakness on the part of the Persian ruler created a power vacuum, which the sheiks immediately took advantage of. As religious individuals, they increased religious shows such as Ta'ziyah. Unlike what happened in the period of Fath Ali Shah, in which only the wealthy aristocrats and the rich participated in the financing of the shows, in this period we witness the participation of every social stratum (even the worthy poor) since the deep imprint of sacredness that the sheiks gave to the spectacle produced in every individual the want to participate in such an extraordinarily important event.

A fair amount of valuable information and sources about Persia of this period have been recovered for us by various European travelers and cultural ambassadors who wrote about Persian customs of the time. A character of particular

---

[81] Peace treaty between Persia and Russia, signed in 1813

[82] Peace treaty between Persia and Russia, signed in 1828.

importance, of which many of his sources have come down to us, is the Count de Sercey.[83] French ambassador to Tehran, de Sercey, in his memorial, scrupulously noted various customs.

With regard to the theater, he noted that Persian actors also used to dress in women's clothes (recall that women were not allowed to act with men). Another aspect dealt with by the French attends to the competition that existed between the aristocrats in building an ever more majestic Tekeyeh. In a religious society, which produced a lot of space to the Ta'ziyah, those who contributed better than the others to the greatness of these shows were undoubtedly regarded with special attention.

The Ta'ziyah during the reign of Naser Al-Din Shah. (1848 – 1896)

During the reign of Naser Al-Din Shah, it is evident that foreign influence, particularly from Europe, gradually gained greater control over the Persian monarchy. If initially, the only power that enjoyed political privileges was England, later the presence of the French and Russian governments was also noted. These European powers had control over Persian resources and wealth, which they acquired and exploited at low costs, primarily due to the vulnerability of the local economy. It is in this context that a decisive individual makes his appearance: the vizier Amir Kabir.[84]

A very significant character, he had even married the Shah's sister. Amir Kabir attempted to implement a policy to influence the king to expel Europeans from Persian territory.

---

83 Count de Sercey, translator Ehsan Eshraghi, *Persia in 1839-1840*, (Tehran, SoKhan, 2010), 157-158.

84 Yaghub Azhand, *Theatre of the Qajars*, (Namāyish dar dawrah-i Qājār), 39-40.

As his first political act, he established the borders of his country with the Ottoman Empire. For centuries, there had never been a clearly defined border between the two countries. In a second instance, he attempted to withhold the abundant natural resources of Persia from the Europeans. According to Amir, the existing agreements were unfavorable for Persia, as they forced the country to accept meager prices due to fear of upsetting the Europeans. Persia should not have been compelled to sell off or even give away these valuable resources, as they rightfully belonged to the Persian people. Naser Al Din Shah was aware of the qualities, wisdom, and firmness of his brother-in-law vizier. Whenever he was capable, he would follow his advice and attempt to implement an anti-European policy.

However, the immense economic and military power of the governments of London and Paris posed a formidable challenge. The ruler of Persia, despite his desire to align with his vizier's policies, often found himself compelled to act differently. Concerned about the vizier's detrimental influence, the British and French governments resorted to the assassination of Amir Kabir as a means to resolve the issue. Also, during this period, we witnessed the cession of the Transoxiana region to Russia and the independence of Afghanistan.

As a first political act, the Shah sanctioned the borders of his country with the Ottoman Empire, since for centuries a real and precise border between the two countries had never existed. He used to go in fact to the Golestan place,[85] or to the Shah Abdul Azim.[86] The sovereign made three trips to Europe thanks to which he became aware of present forms of entertainment. This passion for the world of theatre and

---

[85] It is the historical residence of the Qajar royal dynasty, located in Tehran.

[86] Located in Rey, Persia, it contains the tomb of 'Abdul' Adhīm ibn 'Abdillah al-Hasani (Shah Abdol Azim).

entertainment led him to embark on a truly innovative project for a ruler of Persia: a journey around the world to learn about the customs and traditions of foreign countries. It was a revolutionary gesture since, until then, there had never been a sovereign who had departed from his own country. The sovereign made three trips to Europe, where he became acquainted with the latest forms of entertainment, including operas and ballets.

Once back in Persia, Naser Al-Din Shah ordered the construction of a truly unparalleled Tekyeh. Inspired by the Royal Albert Hall in London and the amphitheater in Verona, the Dowlat Tekyeh was built. It was so large that it could accommodate up to 20,000 people. Given Naser Al-Din Shah's obsessive attention to detail, the buildings he constructed featured elaborate and intricate ornaments, capable of enchanting visitors and spectators of these magnificent structures.

It is fascinating to underline how the theatre has not always held the same importance for the sovereign. Before becoming king, Naser Ad Din Shah had shown a strong reluctance and lack of interest in entertainment and various forms of theatre. After ascending to the throne and traveling across Europe, he appeared to have a change of heart on this issue. Most likely, this was due to the fact that he perceived in the display a form of propaganda that showcased the greatness, magnificence, and non-backwardness of Persia, particularly to the Persian population and to foreign countries.

The plays of this period show an increasing tendency towards the unreal, excessively vulgar language, or religious fanaticism. Precisely for this reason, some prominent individuals, including the aforementioned Amir Kabir, expressed their disagreement with the Ta'ziyah and avoided attending the shows as much as possible. The vizier adopted this stance because he was concerned that excessive artificiality and vulgarity over time could turn the religious aspect of Islam into a mere theatrical show. This, in turn, could potentially lead people to lose their faith and undermine the integrity of Islam itself. The immune response of the religious authorities and the people was not long in coming. Amir Kabir was often portrayed as a radical opponent of Persian traditions, who, among other things, sought to strip the people of Persia of their primary source of entertainment. The insistence and vehemence with which Amir Kabir was attacked, as well as his political loneliness, lead him to renounce his claims about Ta'ziyah, enabling the people and religious authorities to continue to experience this form of entertainment as they wished.[87]

It must be said that in this period, given the extensive journeys to European countries, Ta'ziyah assumed important characteristics that demonstrate the influence of the European theater. Scenography, music, the role of the supervisor, costumes, and many of the European canons were transplanted into the Persian show which in this period reaches the peak of its wealth and the fulfillment of a formative path. It should be noted that the greater knowledge of Europeans and their traditions convinced the people of Persia that they would end up in hell while the Persians, children of the just law, were in paradise. This is also noticeable in the show as whenever a villain or antagonist appears; they are presented in European clothing; while those who are on the side of the righteous are sent on stage in Persian dress.

---

[87] Yaghub Azhand, *Theatre of the Qajars*, (Namāyish dar dawrah-i Qājār), 40-41.

The Ta'ziyah during the reign of Mozafar al-din Shah (1896 – 1907)

Towards the end of the nineteenth century, during the reign of Mozafar Al-Din Shah, the influx of European travelers to eastern countries, including Persia, continued without interruption. Noteworthy are the French visitors Henry D'Allemagne and Eugène Aubin.

The first, in his memoirs, writes about the Persian show, highlighting, once again, the importance of Ta'ziyah and Tekeyeh. He notes that in the audience of the shows of this period, people are divided into two spaces: on one side, to the left, are the women, while on the other side, to the right, and divided by a corridor in which guards are stationed, the men are to be found.[88]

The importance of Ta'ziyah is so widespread that the French author even writes that he met about two hundred Moin ol boka (directors of Ta'ziyah) every day. Moving outside the capital, Aubin records how he witnessed forms of Ta'ziyah in cemeteries (as in the village of Gom), where actors staged plays about the deaths of some Islamic saints. Focusing on the origin of Ta'ziyah, Aubin specifies that it dates back to the Safavid period.

Like D'Allemagne he writes down valuable information on the Moin ol boka. These were elderly men, with thick, styled beards, who had at least thirty-seven years of theatrical experience behind them. They also acted as heralds for successful shows as they were frequently seen at crossroads and in historic squares with scrolls and sticks announcing the imminence of academic performance.[89]

---

[88] Hanry D'Allemagne, translator Homayun, *the travel memory from Khorasan to Bakhtiari*, (Tehran, Frahvashi, 1999), 272.
[89] Henry D'Allemagne, translator Homayun, *Travel memoirs from Khorasan to Bakhtiari*, 271-272.

Fig. 6. Mirza Mohammad Bagher Mo'in-ol-Boka (center) with manuscripts in hand during a shabih'khani in Tekyeh Dowlat, Golestan Place, Qajar period.

As the vizier Amir Kabir had already guessed some time before, the Ta'ziyah had assumed a decidedly vulgar aspect and language; during the reign of Mozafar Al-Din Shah, this situation grew more and more.

An example of vulgarity, as related by Etemad Al-Soltan, and dating back to 1882, involves one in which, in the Seyed Hasan Kashi mosque, a Rozeh Khan, instead of reciting important verses on the lives of Islamic saints, began to joke about them and transform a place sacred in a very vulgar square.[90]

Among the reasons that prevented the progressive development of Ta'ziyah , after the period of the reign of Mozafar Aldin Shah, we can identify three main ones:

- Importation of European theatre culture into Persia;

- Employment of amateurs to make the Ta'ziyah;

- the entry of Persian comedy beginning with the Tekyeh.

---

[90] It is the largest and most famous Qajar-era mosque in Isfahan.

The form of the Ta'ziyah

In the Ta'ziyah there are in common three critical elements: gestures, music, and words. As in all theatrical genres, even in this one, we possess the presence of the effective component as opposed to the negative one, the protagonist against the antagonist. Usually, the Saints and their families were the positive elements and wore white or green clothing. Alternatively, potential enemies always wore red. The saints always sang in the minor key while the enemies sang in the major chord.

It must be remembered that there were two diverse types of Ta'ziyah.[91]

1. In Ta'ziyah Mozhek (literally: "Ridiculous Ta'ziyah"), the protagonists mostly engaged in playful banter with the principal actors portraying the role of enemies. In this genre, there were always many exaggerations and caricatures, both in the dialogue and in the movements.

2. In Taziye zanane (literally: "Ta'ziyah for women"), both the actors and spectators were women. This type of theater was performed in the homes and gardens of aristocratic individuals.

The earliest information we undoubtedly possess is from the period of Fath Ali Shah.

Azdol Dole in his History of Azodi[92] writes of the reigns of Agha Mohammad Khan, Mohammad Shah, and Fath Ali Shah and says that:

> In the court of Fath Ali Shah there was a woman known as the little lady who managed other women. The woman was exceptionally

---

[91] Bahram Beyzaee, *Theatre in Iran*, [Namāyish dar Īrān], 160-162.
[92] Azod ol doleh, *History of Azodi*, [Tārīkh-i 'Azụdī], (Tehran, Abdol Hoseyn Navaee, 1977).

> tall; she lined up the others and commanded them. At Ashura time, she was running the Ta'ziyah and preparing everything to do with the show with their help.[93]

In this specimen of Ta'ziyah the actresses were solely women and they also played the male roles, putting on their faces and altering their voices. Usually, this form of Ta'ziyah was made in the houses and courtyards of the king.[94]

As mentioned earlier, during the reign of Naser Al-din Shah, women helped Ta'ziyah workers clean and distribute tea and other items that the production offered for drinking or eating.

Fig. 7. Center older Mirza Mohammad Bagher Mo'in-ol-Boka, Golestan Place, Qajar period

Regardless of the theatrical festivals, this spectacle is still performed in Persia in a period between April and May, on the anniversary of Husayn's death. It should also be noted that the Ta'ziyah was not only an Islamic play, but the creativity of various artists brought many other elements of

[93] Ibid, 45-46.
[94] Ibid, 160-161.

Persian culture into this theatrical form until it finally became a true symbol of the country's culture. Today, we can see how playwrights take the structure of the ta'ziyah as a starting point to adapt modern plays in which, however, the ancient myths of the ta'ziyah are clearly visible.

From the Middle Ages to the sixteenth century, there were widespread plays in Europe called Mystères or Mysteries, which contained structural elements close to Ta'ziyah. It should be remembered that during this period many travelers from the West visited Persia and also many merchants and artists from Persia came to various European countries. It can be assumed that there was a cultural exchange and mutual influence of spectacular forms, which in Europe were determined by curiosity and interest in everything that seemed exotic. The merchants who traveled in both directions learned about the customs and festive habits of the Persian people by attending the spectacles: After their return to Europe, they provided reports and chronicles to the citizens of their countries.

Acting in the Ta'ziyah

Before we begin to explain the form of recitation in the Ta'ziyah, we need to know some of its keywords. The term Shabih Khan, performer of the Ta'ziyah, comes from the words Shabih, which means to look, and Khan, which means reader, meaning that a person, the Shabih Khan, acted in place of a saint or an enemy.

The actors of the Ta'ziyah are therefore divided into two specific camps: the Olia Khan and the Ashghia Khan. The former embody the saints and the latter the enemies.

The group of Olia Khanan is equally divided into other sections:[95] those who act in place of the Imams; those who act in place of champions; those who act in place of women; and those who act in place of the children.

Fig. 8. Actor of Ta'ziyah, Golestan Place, Qajar period.

Alternatively, the Ashghia Khan can be divided into four groups:[96] the one that recites instead of the Shemr; Takht Khan, or the kings of enemies or their governors; Mokhalef Khan, those who played the part of angels and spirits; and enemy soldiers.

Usually, these actors weren't famous. The Ta'ziyah's producers preferred those who had a very beautiful and strong voice; usually, those who acted in place of the saints

---

[95] Enayat Allah Shahidi, Research in *Ta'ziyah h and Ta'ziyah h Khani*, [Pizhuhishī dar ta'zīyah va ta'zīyah'khvānī : az āghāz tā pāyān-i dawrah-'i Qājār dar Tihrān],(Daftar-i Pizhuhish'hā-yi Farhangī : Kumīsiyūn- i Millī-i Yūniskū dar Īrān, 2002), 325.

[96] Ibid.

had to be tall and good-looking. Instead, those who acted for the enemies had to have a mean face and a powerful voice.[97]

Men were chosen who usually had different occupations and came from different cities. They had to physically resemble the character they were to play. For example, an actor who was to take Husayn's place had to have an attractive, unshaven face. In general, we can say the physical properties of the actors were very important to get a role in the plays.[98]

Young actors who wanted to start performing the Ta'ziyah were only exposed to one type of Ta'ziyah and typically focused on practicing the same role repeatedly. The Ta'ziyah's actors, as soon as they stepped on stage, forgot they were acting and their performance was extremely naturalistic, as the Moin ol Boka had tried to orchestrate it.[99]

Ta'ziyah costumes and accessories

Usually, the head of the Ta'ziyah prepares the clothes and accessories for the scene. At the end of the preparation period, the Ta'ziyah stores them for the following year. As mentioned, the actors in the Ta'ziyah were divided into two main groups: the saints and the enemies. Saints usually had on white, green, and brown clothing, while enemies wore red and black clothing.[100]

However, all of the actors were dressed in their own unique style, making them instantly identifiable. For example, Husayn or the other Imams wore a green cape, black trousers, and a white shirt.[101]

---

[97] Yaghub Azhand, *Theatre of the Qajars*,(Namāyish dar dawrah-i Qājār), 92-93.
[98] Ibid 94-95.
[99] Ibid 96-98.
[100] Ibid 102.
[101] Ibid.

Fig. 9. Mirza Mohammad Bagher Mo'in-ol-Boka with his manuscripts among actors in costume, Golestan Place, Qajar period.

It is interesting to know that in the Qajar period the governors and ministries of the enemies usually dressed in contemporary European fashion and, sometimes, were dressed in brown cape with a shirt and trousers, both brown. Angels, on the other hand, always wore white robes.[102]

The props they used on stage were a mirror, a Turkish stone ring, a papyrus, a coffin, a bowl of water, boots, a sword, a knife, a severed hand, books, rose water, carpets, a dead body, and some animals, like horses, lions, camels, sheep, and elephants.[103]

These clothes and accessories acquired symbolic meaning. For example, if they placed a glass of water on the ground, it was to be understood as the symbol of a river called Furat.[104]

---

[102] Ibid 103-104.

[103] Ibid 103.

[104] An important technique in the Ta'ziyah is the agreements that the actors make with the spectators during the performance

Texts and music by Ta'ziyah

Almost all of the Ta'ziyah's lyrics were written by anonymous authors. In their centuries-old evolution, theatrical scripts have taken the form of poetry and occasionally prose. The poems were simple, and the audience easily understood them. The language of writing was not always Persian; indeed every so often it was Turkish or Arabic.[105]

If we analyze the texts of the Ta'ziyah, we can see that the classic structure of a screenplay is missing. Indeed, the poems lend themselves to traditional literature. However, when the script was enacted by the actors, one could witness an exceptionally fascinating spectacle.

Among all the historical religious texts that told the story of Kerbela, *Rozat ol shohada* was an important book and it was written by Husayn Vaez Kashefi in 1503. This text tells the story of Kerbela and other Islamic saints.[106]

Each Ta'ziyah is normally structured into three parts.

1. Prologue: A secondary Ta'ziyah that tells diverse stories, not just religious ones.

2. The Ta'ziyah's main text.

3. Gushe: an independent type of Ta'ziyah that has evolved from the original Ta'ziyah.

In this type of Ta'ziyah, we can observe the emergence of various themes, including love, which can bring the performance closer to comedic elements. When a Ta'ziyah became comedic, it was because the saints wanted to mock their enemies. This is the case of the Ta'ziyah mozhek (which translates to "ridiculous Ta'ziyah"), in which the actors primarily engage in playful banter with other actors

---

[105] Yaghub Azhand, *Theatre of the Qajars*,(Namāyish dar dawrah-i Qājār), 109-110.
[106] Ibid 110-111

portraying the role of enemies. In this genre, there are often many exaggerations and caricatures, both in the dialogues and in the movements.

Ta'ziyah is one of the major forms of performance in Persia that can be easily followed and understood by the population. A very important reason for the development of Ta'ziyah is its language. Initially, Ta'ziyah used the language of the people, but later it transitioned to an integrated linguistic register that embraced the lexicon and expressive forms of literature, such as similes, metaphors, and hyperbole. The public perceived and even appreciated this form of greater artistic elaboration.

Music can be considered an important element that allowed Ta'ziyah to become the main form of Persian entertainment. Persian music developed in parallel with Ta'ziyah.

Ruh Allah Khalegi,[107] a great Persian musician, in his book entitled *History of Persian Music*, says:

> The Ta'ziyah was an important reason for saving some Persian songs. In the Ta'ziyah people instantly accepted a person who had a good voice. Indeed, when a young man had a good voice, the Ta'ziyah's directors promptly accepted him to star in the Ta'ziyah. Teachers gave him some lessons and then recited [...]. It is clear that famous singers have sprung from the heart of this show.[108]

We can say the Ta'ziyah was an integrated show of poetry, music, and history. The chief musical instruments are drums,

---

[107] Khaleghi, born 1906 in Kerman, Iran and died November 12, 1965 in Salzburg, was a prominent Persian musician, composer, conductor and author.

[108] Ruh ollah Khaleghi, *History of Persian Music*, [Sarguzasht-i mūsīqī-i Īrān], (Tehran Safi ali Shah, 1975), 348.

cymbals, flutes, trombones, trumpets, saxophone, clarinets, and tubas.

In a society that was gradually embracing Western influences, participation in the Ta'ziyah played a crucial role in transforming women's entertainment. For many centuries after the advent of Islam, most women had lived primarily within the confines of their homes, fulfilling the role of housewives. However, during this period, they gradually started to venture outside and actively engage in public life.

The play mainly featured performances aimed at a female audience. The women repeatedly entered before the men and sat down. Sometimes, quarrels and screams would break out among the women who were vying for the best seats, leading to the intervention of the attendants.

Ta'ziyah in some cities: Borujerd, Mashhad, Tehran

Borujerd is quite an old city that has always had spectacular forms since the Safavid times, like the ta'ziyah called Khere Giri. Early in the morning, before dawn, some people went to the public bath in trousers, barefoot and shirtless. The owner of the bath prepared a bowl of water made of earth and rose water before their arrival. As soon as the people entered the bath, they hit each other on the head and chest, cried, and called the name of Husayn. At the end of this ritual spectacle, the bath attendant offered breakfast to the participants.

From the first day of the month of Muharram until the tenth day, called Ashura,[109] people covered all the walls of a room of the house with black fabric and placed a Menbar (pulpit) with lots of candles on it.

---

[109] In the Islamic calendar, Ashura indicates the 10th of the month of Muharram, which is an important religious festival.

In the period of Ashura, those who asked God for something in the month participated in this spectacular form that comes from the Ta'ziyah. One person would go to forty houses and place forty candles, and until this ritual was finished the petitioner could not speak. During these ten days, all the candles remained lit. When the night of the tenth day came, people blew out candles to represent Husayn's death.

If at the end of the year, the postulant obtained what he had requested from God, the first of Muharram of the following year he set up the room again to ask for graces for others. The room therefore was considered Sagha Khane.[110] If at the end of the year the postulant obtained what he had requested from God, on the first of Muharram of the following year he set up the room again to ask for graces for others.[111]

As mentioned, in sacred months such as Muharram and Safar, in almost all the cities of Persia there were successful shows of a religious subject, especially the Ta'ziyah. During Ta'ziyah season, the king and the governor of the city allocated money for performances. The last eight lines of Document 4 (which dates back to the reign of Fath Ali Shah)

---

[110] In Persian architecture, in the street, the places created by the inhabitants who put water for the people.

[111] I obtained this information personally by interviewing the people in charge of the representation.

Fig. 10. Saghakhaneh, Borujerd, The photo was taken by the author himself.

mention the money which by executive order of the Shah had to be allocated. The document, under the official title of a contribution from the year 1830 of the village of Kheshtiank,[112] and stamped with the name of King Fath Ali Shah, speaks of the governor and other clerics of the city who contributed to the repair of a mosque called the Sultan mosque, reads:

"[...] for the workers of the local mosque sixty Tuman[113] [...], and to make Ta'ziyah in the period of Ashura fifteen Tuman for a week [...]."

---

112 Village in rural district of Goodarzi province of Lorestan, Persia.

113 Iran's currency.

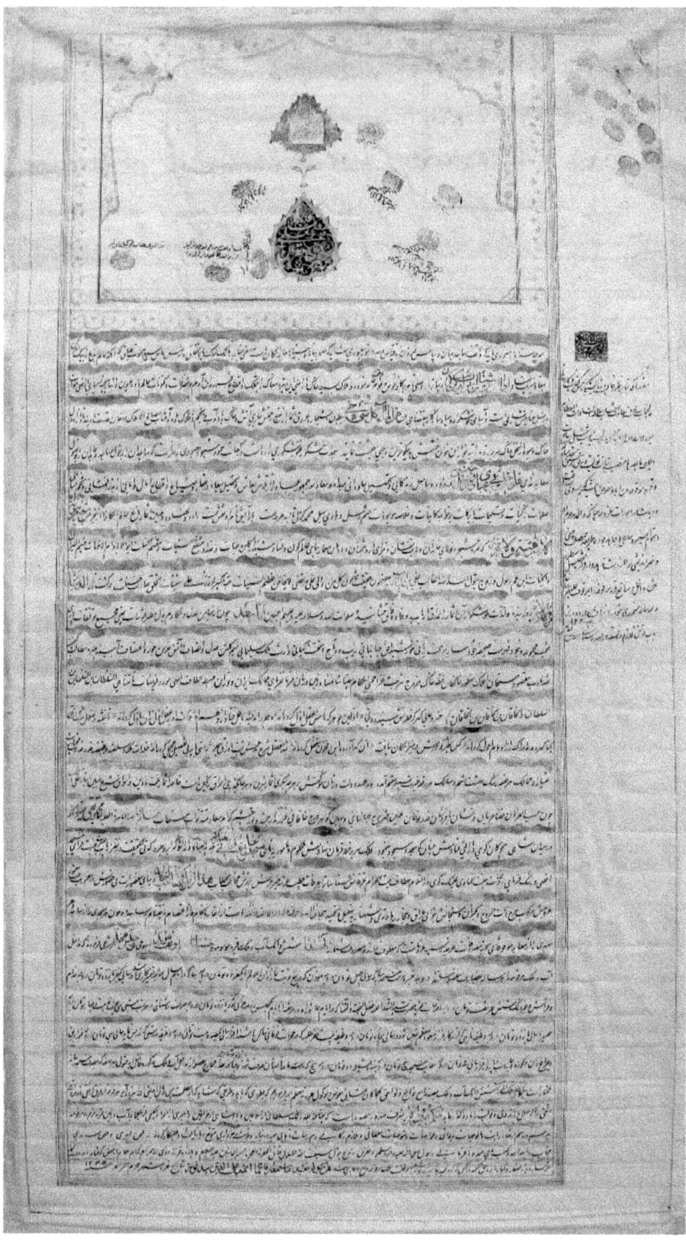

Fig. 11. Vaghf nameh, borujerd cultural heritage department, 1830.

Mashhad is an ancient city and renowned place of worship, boasting a centuries-old tradition of spectacular customs. After the discovery of the tomb of Imam Reza in Mashhad, it has become a primary destination for pilgrimages.

In the Safavid period people went to Mashhad to pray, and on such occasions, of course, many funeral rites and religious rituals were performed.

The first document that speaks of a spectacular shape compared to the Ta'ziyah is dated 1604 and concerns the Ashura of that year. The document records the considerable expenses incurred for the preparation of a public bath and the fact that this bath must be closed on a particular date (Ashura) because on that day the Rozeh Khani will be performed in front of the bath.

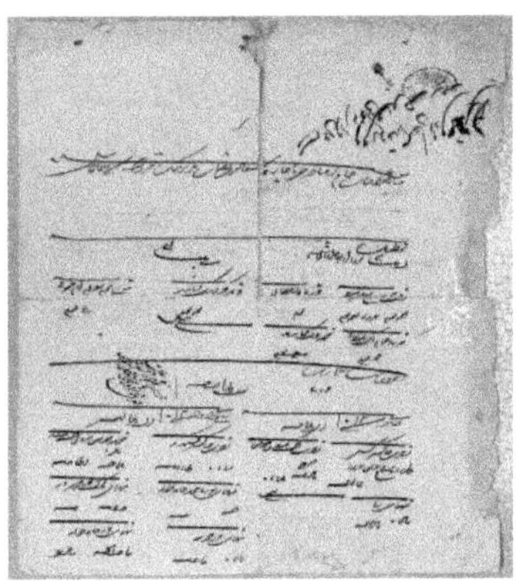

Fig. 12. The first handwritten document of Roze khani (The initial form of Ta'ziyah), Astan Quds Razavi library and archive, 1604.

The second important document from 1658 speaks of the expenses incurred by the residents of an area of Mashhad in the first ten days of the month of Muharram for funeral rites, and explains how much was paid for the people who performed the Roze Khani.

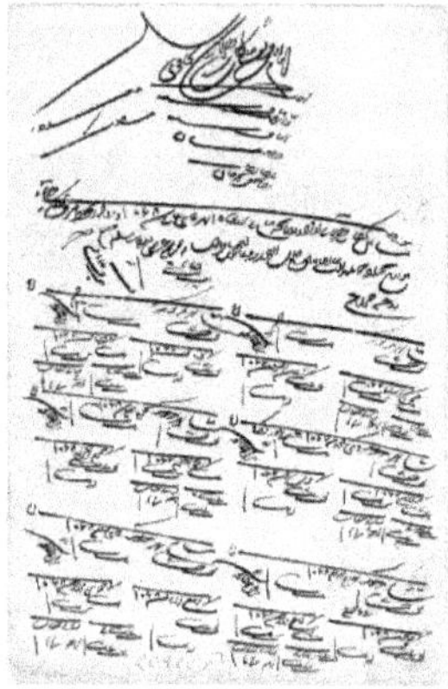

Fig. 13. Handwritten document of Roze khani in Mashhad, Astan Quds Razavi library and archive, 1658.

Once Agha Mohammad Khan came to power, he chose Tehran as his capital for strategic reasons. As mentioned above, the wars during his reign left no room for the development of artistic activities, and if there were performances, it was only on the initiative of the people. After him, and under the reign of Fath Ali Shah, on the other hand, performances increased, as they did during the reign of Naser al-din Shah, which was especially fundamental for the development of the ta'ziyah.

During the reign of Naser al-din Shah, there was a newspaper called *Iran*[114] which was published by Etemad ol Saltane. The main part of this newspaper contained the schedule of the Shah for his institutional obligations. In different numbers you can follow the news of events that took place in the ruler's palace on his initiative. In issue 914 of this journal, Etemad Ol Saltaneh writes on the front page:

> As we reported in the previous issue, on Thursday, the second day of the month of

[114] Journal active during the reign of Naser al din Shah with responsibility for Etemad ol Saltaneh. It began to be printed in 1871.

> Muharram, the great king went to his villa in the Sherman area. On Sunday, the fifth of the month of Muharram, several groups began to make aliyah right in front of the villa. The performances were magnificent. Every the evening, the storytellers and actors of the Ta'ziyah came and told of the sufferings of the family of the saints and especially the family of Husayn. On the fourteenth of the same month, we finished the production of the Ta'ziyah, and the king gave many things to the actors and producers.

We know that ten days of the month of Muharram were dedicated to this spectacle, but we cannot say that the Ta'ziyah was interesting for all of the clergy and governors.

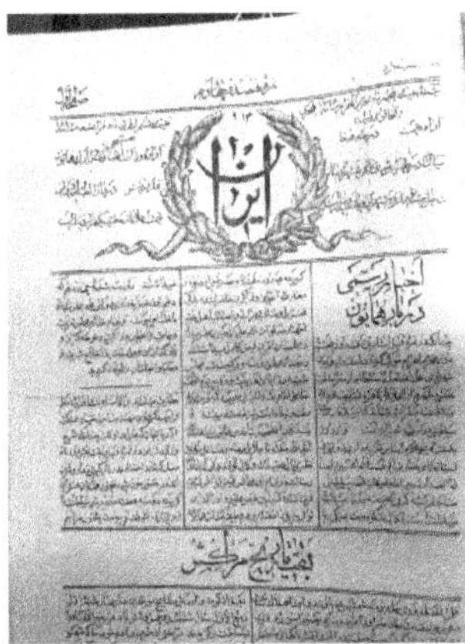

Fig. 14.Newspaper of Iran, number 914, Haram Shah Abdol Azim Library and Archive, Tehran, June 25, 1897.

Some clergymen thought that the Ta'ziyah destroyed Islam and that depicting the lives of saints was harmful and blasphemous. On 31 January, 1893, the Ta'ziyah of Ghasem was scheduled to escape from the principal mosque of Shiraz, but the Sheykh of the mosque and the other religious did not enable the actors to enter and it was necessary to resort to the mediation work of the local governor to resolve the problem.[115]

Presumably in some cities, the Ta'ziyah was banned for a period, but after two years, Rokn al Dole, nephew of Naser al-Din Din Shah, who remained governor of Kerman and Shiraz, unblocked the regulations against the Ta'ziyah.

After the resistance of some religious people against the creation of the Ta'ziyah, there were, in addition, some intellectuals who were against it. Among them some scholars who recognized European theater well, like Akhund Zade,[116] thought that the Ta'ziyah's production was based on exaggerated habits contrary to the Islamic religion and also criticized the poor preparation and rough performances of the actors, as well as the vulgarity of the scripts, inadequate for the celebration of saints.[117]

Another Persian scholar of that period, Mirza Agha Tabrizi,[118] explicitly criticizes the Ta'ziyah's audience and writes:

> For many days they make themselves up like women, and prepare their hair because they want to go and see the Ta'ziyah. They sit in front of the women who have enveloped their heads. When it's hot, they start wiping their sweaty faces, maybe they cough; instead, when young people look at these things they

---

[115] Mohamad Hasan Khan Etemad ol saltaneh, *Journal of Memories*, [Khạtirāt-i I'timād al-Saḷtanah], (Tehran, Amir kabir, 1893), n: 422.
[116] (12 1812 –1878) was an Azerbaijani writer.
[117] Yaghub Azhand, *Theatre of the Qajars*,(Namāyish dar dawrah-i Qājār), 133-136.
[118] He was the first Persian writer to have written a script in the classical form of the Persian language.

> think that women treasure them and want to allude to something. This is our Ta'ziyah.[119]

Some governors and government officials were not in favor of the Ta'ziyah's preparation of performances, and one of the most prominent of these opponents was Etemad ol Saltaneh, who writes in his diary:

> On the fourth day of the month of Muharram (November 25, 1881) there was a Ta'ziyah on Fatima. This Ta'ziyah was very vulgar. The actors barked like dogs. The spectators were not crying, but laughing. The people who heard their voices from afar said that not even in a comedy do you ever hear such loud laughter.[120]

If we want to narrate its story from its dawn to its sunset's hour, we can say the Ta'ziyah begins in the Safavid period with spectacular religious forms such as Rozeh Khani and Daste Garden, etc. Then, in the funeral rites, there was a spectacular change: the transition from storytelling to acting practice. Progressively, animated forms and dialogues were added to the narrative. Later with the addition of spectacular techniques, the play came to resemble a theatrical performance.

In the last years of the Safavid government, we can follow the definition of a religious dramaturgical structure, and in the years of the transition from the Safavid government to the

---

[119] It is from a manuscript by Mirza Agha Tabrizi, *Four plays and Ehical book*, [Chahār tiyātr], (Tabriz, Ibn Sina, 1976).

[120] Mohamad Hasan Khan Etemad ol saltaneh, *Journal of Memories*, [Khạtirāt-i I'timād al-Saḷtanah[, 32.

Fig.15. Mirza Mohammad Bagher Mo'in-ol-Boka (standing, front, second from right), Tekyeh Dowlat, Golestan Place, Qajar period.

Qajar government, we are witnessing the development of numerous scripts like the Rozat ol shahada for which permanent jobs are created for those who have to produce the play. As soon as we arrive at the period of the reign of Naser al-din Shah, the established theatres, called Tekieh, are born, which in turn enrich this theatrical form.

As long as the king was young, he didn't pay attention to shows. However, as he grew older, it became his passion, and he started organizing splendid religious shows. He even built a large theater where Ta'ziyah performances were usually held. It is possible that this was intended as a way of advertising his government, and so the Ta'ziyah assumed its main form. Then, after the death of Naser al-din Shah, the Ta'ziyah no longer had a great patron. In the period of the Constitutional Revolution, there was a profound change in the Persian mentality, which by then had substantially adapted to European models.

The Qajar period was a time when Europeans visited Iran frequently. Meanwhile, the information provided by Europeans about Persian play forms provides us with many important details of Iranian plays. It also reflects the perspective of Westerners on Iran's plays.

Cornelis de Bruijn (1652 – 1726 or 1727) was a Dutch painter, writer, and traveler. In 1704 he arrived in Persia, where he remained for a long period. There he writes his travel memoir, in which he discusses the funeral rite of Kerbela, the death of Husayn, indicating that the latter and his friends totaled seventy-two and were highly respected by the people.

He explains the annual funeral rites performed for Husayn and Ali, and provides additional information about the coffins used during these funerals. He explains that people symbolically carried the body and head of saints using wax reproductions. He tells us the Persians are very good at this simulation and, in particular, in the practice of modeling the bodies of saints with wax. He tells us about the people who carried the modeled body of Husayn in this way: "The inside of Husayn's body was abandoned; there was someone who made the body move, people offered gifts, and he too gave a coin of silver to the people, and the people thought that silver was sacred."[121]

Carsten Neibuhr (March 17, 1733 - April 26, 1815) was a German mathematician, cartographer and explorer in the service of the Danish state. He came to Persia when Karim Khan was the king of Persia. In his report about him we can find very useful information, especially about the island of Khark. He writes that at that time there were Shiites and Sunnis in Khark and for this reason the government decided to expel from the cities the Shiites who practiced rituals. But on the day of Ashura, the Shiites returned to the city and

[121] Corneille Le Brun, *Voyages de Corneille Le Brun Per la Moscovie en Perse*, (Amsterdam, Freres Wetstein, 1718), 215-217.

went to the main square, where they celebrated their rites, especially the Ta'ziyah.[122]

Fig. 16. An example for Ta'ziyah, tekiya kamraniye, north of Tehran, Golestan Place, Qajar period.

Neibuhr claims that everyone came to the square weeping and beating their chests, invoking "Husayn." Those who played Yazid's[123] role and those of his soldiers dressed in red and as soon as they entered the square they began to pretend they were seeking someone. When Husayn came in, they went fighting him. One of Husayn's soldiers who played the role of Ghasem, a noble and valiant knight, fell from his horse and wanted to get up to continue fighting, but his daughters began crying, asking for an end to the battle for fear of losing their father. Another main character of Kerbala is named Abu Alfazl.[124] Yazid's soldiers cut off his hands while he was fetching water for the children and women. Neibuhr testifies in his writings that this scene was particularly well done. Not all of the performers, according to

---

122 Carsten Neibuhr, translator Parviz Rajabi, *Travel memoirs*, (Tehran Tuka, 1975), 190.

123 Yazid (645-683), Arab Caliph.

124 Abu al fazl (647-680), son of Ali, first Shi'ite Imam.

him, were good actors. However, the ones who portrayed the character of Abu Alfazl were highly popular among the audience. The music was only performed by the cymbals that accompanied Husayn's vocals.

While Yazid had a great many, Husayn had only seventy-two soldiers. Despite this, and every so often, Husayn's soldiers won the battles, although in the end all were killed, including Husayn; and later Yazid's soldiers also captured their families. In another part of the square, Yazid is sitting on a chair talking to a European next to him, an ambassador of Greece who wants to intercede so as not to have Husayn killed, but Yazid, even before delivering him an audience, gives orders to kill him too.[125]

This information provided to us by Neibuhr is among the earliest evidence regarding Ta'ziyah as a theatrical performance; however, the author does not inform us whether the actors of Ta'ziyah acted following a theatrical text or not.

James Morier (1780-1849) was an English politician and writer; he lived for several years in Persia where he observed Persian customs. The result of his travels in Persia is a book called *The Adventures of Haji Baba of Isfahan.*

In one of his travel letters, he speaks of the Ta'ziyah, which he attends near a sacred tomb; Morier says people were seated around the actors, and Indian soldiers were also present along with the British ambassadors. It began with Roze Khani[126] and continued with Sine zani,[127] at the end of

125 Carsten Neibuhr, traduttore Parviz Rajabi, *Carsten Neibuhr's travelogue,*[Safarnāmah-'i Kārstin Nībūr], (Tehran, Tuka, 1975),190-191.

126 One or, sometimes, two people, probably The Sheykh or a religious, told or sang an episode of the religious tradition of Islam, entitled Kerbela.This kind of performance probably emerged after the publication of Rozat ol shohada, an important book on Ta'ziyah , written by Hoseyn Vaez Kashefi in 1503. This text tells the story of Kerbela' and other Islamic saints.Basically, this spectacular custom took place in squares,

which a Ta'ziyah was performed which spoke of the death of Husayn. There is a particularly important passage of Morier's testimony when speaking of this Ta'ziyah, where he says the actors held a handwritten script and acted with the help of a text, referring to the moment when Husayn and his soldiers die thirsty. At that point five Saghi would enter the scene with wineskins filled with water, to show Husayn's thirst.[128]

Fig. 17. Ta'ziyah moslem's children, One of the Tehran's Tekiyeh, Golestan Place, Qajar period.

The second rite that Morier testifies to having seen was held the following day and took place inside the house of a governor. This suggests that the religious performances were also held in personal homes or in castles, indicating that the master came from a noble or royal family. In fact, the nobles

streets,mosque , markets, in the presence of many people and the Roze Khan sat on the Minbar or on a chair. The people stood around him while he told the stories of the book of Rozat ol shohada with spectacular gestures, driving those present to emotion and tears.

127 Religious ceremonies, people beat their chests with their hands and express their grief in this way.

128 James Morier, translator Abolghasem Seri, *Travel memoirs*, (Tehran, Tus, 2007), 232-233.

in that period, to show their power, tried to enjoy splendid and very expensive shows made at their expense.[129]

Morier says the same shows were made that day as the day before. In this scene, Yazid's interpreter sits with three other actors, all dressed as Europeans, while soldiers arrive carrying Husayn's son, Zayn al-Abedin.[130] Yazid irritates them. At this precise moment one of the people staying with Yazid, the Greek ambassador, wants to save him but Yazid gives the order to kill him. And at this point, Morier reports, viewers are crying.[131]

Morier equally tells us that on the last day of the funeral celebrated in front of the king, a very odd thing happens: the Ta'ziyah is interrupted because the actor who was supposed to play the role of Husayn doesn't show up; the previous day in a small village near Isfahan, the Shimr,[132] during a similar performance, had really cut off the head of the one who played the role of Husayn, so the actor, recognizing what typically happened to his unfortunate colleague there, was afraid of the act.[133]

Morier, in the subsequent volume of his travel memoirs, is more specific about Persian performances than in the first. The king of Persia invites him to see the Ta'ziyah that typically takes place in the main square, right in front of the king's castle. Morier writes that, in ten days, a number of shows are held on the life of Husayn depicting the period from the exit from Madineh to Kerbela. Every day a different episode is represented: large black tents, called Tekie, are set up in the square. The nobles and the common people cover the expenses for the ten days for the sacredness of the event. Each tent has a Roze Khan, and the sound of music is always

---

[129] Ibid 233

[130] Zayn al-Abidin: the fourth Shia Imam.

[131] Ibid 234.

[132] Shimr was an Arab military who killed Husayn ibn Ali.

[133] James Morier, translator Abolghasem Seri, *Travel memoirs*, 234.

heard with instruments such as drums, cymbals, and horns. On the day of Ashura, some nobles from the Qajar dynasty gather in front of the castle door. They remove their shoes and beat their chests as a form of mourning. In one part of the square, they set up two small tents, a symbol of the tents of Husayn.

The Ta'ziyah scene is located in the center of the carpeted plaza. First, two of Ta'ziyah's narrators enter and begin reciting poetry in front of the king. Then, a man enters carrying some skins. Eight other men follow who carry Mohammed's coffin, a drawn one, on which there is a Turban symbolizing Mohammed and next to the Turban are candles. In front of these men are two people carrying two large flags designed with the image of a hand, the symbol of Abu al Fazl. Next approach the people wearing bloody shrouds and carrying a bloody horse, symbol of Zuljanah—all symbols of Husayn's seventy-two soldiers.[134]

Later, an actor called Shabih Khan,[135] had come to start acting. As soon as Husayn dies people cry loudly. Murier says that presently, as Hoseyn fell, the soldiers set fire to Husayn's tents, and the people The who were watching the show up until then had run to beat up the actors playing the role of Yazid's soldiers.

Murier says there is an incredible scene at the end of the play where the bodies of saints are placed on the ground with their heads severed. However, to depict the decapitation, seventy-two people are buried. After that, a person approaches and loudly announces that the show is over. If we want to classify Murier's information, we can list:

---

[134] James Morier, translator Abolghasem Seri, *Travel memoirs*, 219-220.

[135] Shabih Khan, are the Ta'ziyah actors playing instead of Hosein's friends.

1. Roze Khani;

2. Sinezani;

3. Entry of the flags into the square;

4. Arrival of Mohammed's coffin carried on shoulder;

5. Entrance of the drawn horses for the Ta'ziyah;

6. Husayn's soldiers enter;

7. Husayn's horse enters;

8. Entrance of the musicians;

9. Entrance of the actors (Shabih Khan);

10. Display of severed heads;

11. Husayn's family placed in chains;

12. Presence of the written script for the actors.

Chodzko (1804-1891), a Polish politician and orientalist, was one of the most significant travelers during the Qajar period. Before coming to Persia, he had a thorough understanding of the area and was familiar with Persian culture and customs.

He worked for the Russian government and collected thirty-three texts[136] by Ta'ziyah writers. After that, a person comes and loudly announces the show is over. He believes that all the people who work to make the Ta'ziyah do it only to honor god and not to earn money. To better represent the Ta'ziyah, they used props lent by noble families who had the success of the show at heart.[137]

---

136 Thirty three texts by Ta'ziyah. The Polish poet and Iranologist Aleksander Borejko Chodźko (1804 - 1891), following his research on Ta'ziyah , in his book Théâtre persan (Paris, 1878) claimed to have found thirty-three texts of this play.

137 Aleksandro Chodzko, translator Jalal Satari, *The Persian theater*,(Teheran, Faslnameye theatre, 1990),112-113.

Charles Felix Marie Texier (1802-1871) was a French archaeologist, architect, and academic. He says he saw a Ta'ziyah at Golpayegan[138] in the king's castle garden, estimating there were 6,000 people in attendance. He says that day the city was without inhabitants and people were inside the court of the castle of the governor of the city and that they saw an incredible scene: about five thousand people sitting and watching the Ta'ziyah. The performance was about the life of a man that Persians loved dearly. The court was set up like a large theater; the scene was right in the center of the court and the audience was around the scene.[139]

Flandin (1809-1889) was a French Orientalist painter, archaeologist, and explorer. He tells us about a Ta'ziyah performance held in the garden of a grand residence, with the guests seated in said garden, while other individuals positioned themselves on the rooftops of nearby houses. He writes that there were once so many people that they broke through the roofs. According to Flandin that show resembled the religious shows that were done in the medieval period.[140]

Flandin recounts that before starting the show, the Sheikh went to the Minbar and spoke to the crying audience, who were moved by that dramatic story.

The actors used scripts written in poetic form and wore ordinary clothes to create a realistic atmosphere for the show. Script and lyrics had a poetic form. The actors wore everyday clothes to make the show realistic and sometimes borrowed clothes from the population of the cities in which they performed. In another part of his travel diary, he refers to an incident that occurred in a house where many people had gathered to watch a show: the collapse of the roof of the

---

[138] Golpayegan: a sacred city in center of Iran.

[139] Charles Felix Texier, *Description de l'Arménie, la Perse et la Mésopotamie,* (Paris F. Didot frères, 1852), 67.

[140] Eugene Aubin, translator Ali Asgar Saidi, *Today's Iran*, (Tehran, Zavar, 1983), 117-118.

house caused a massacre, and this episode may have encouraged the construction of Tekie specially intended for performances.[141]

Polak (1818-1891) was a German doctor who analyzed the landscapes in his travel report. He argues that celebrating funerals and making the Ta'ziyah are two separate things, that the nobles had no economic problems to build the Tekie but that the people still raised the money and that, if there was no promoter, they asked the nobles for a loan. He says that the performances lasted for ten days and that during this period new stories of the city of Kerbela were performed every day. Some scenes of the Ta'ziyah, as described by Polak, are depicted with such realism that they have a profound impact on both local audiences and foreign travelers. Another interesting aspect for Polak was that the spectators would sometimes quarrel, requiring the intervention of the guards to resolve the resulting scuffles. He also states that in those days the Tekie promoters always provided food and drink for the public.[142]

Edmond O'Donovan (1844-1883) was an Irish correspondent. He gives us unpublished information about a twelve-hour performance of a Ta'ziyah held near Mashhad. The crowd was very large, so the organizers had to relocate the show and move it outside the city. He says he saw another show created solely for the purpose of generating income for the actors. At the end of the Ta'ziyah, some young people in fact collected the money that people offered them.

O'Donvan says that the Ta'ziyah was able to influence the spectators a lot and that once, in fact, in the scene where Yazid's soldiers wanted to kill Hoseyn's son, a man who had

---

141 Ibid 67.

142 Jakob Eduard Polak, translator Keikavus Jahandari, *Iran and Iranian*,[Safarnāmah-i Pūlāk : Irān va Irāniyān], (Tehranm, Kharazmi, 1989), 234-235.

been watching the show up to that point, had taken a sword and had gone to kill the actor who was playing the soldier.[143]

Carla Serena (1824-1884) was an Italian traveler who went to Persia during the period of Naser Al-Din Shah. Her accounts of the shows she attended are very interesting and accurate. She writes that she came to Naser Al-Din Shah after his journey through Europe. He gave the order to build a theatre, called Tekie Dowlat, and that Ta'ziyah was performed in this theatre. She describes it as a splendid palace, furnished with typical Persian carpets and lamps. She tells of the people who sold food and drink outside the Tekie.[144]

According to her, the Ta'ziyah began during the Safavid period with Roze Khani, and later other actors were added to portray the role of saints. Subsequently, and little by little, some actors began inserting improvised dialogue. It is important to underline that Muslim clerics did not want the lives of the saints to be represented, but people crowded the shows anyway, and if at first, the writers did not put their name as the authors of the text of the Ta'ziyah, after a few years signing the text became an honor. [145]

For Carla Serena, the Ta'ziyah recalled medieval religious performances that were very similar to some religious shows held in France and Naples.[146]

The French diplomat Aubin (1863-1931) visited Persia during the Persian Constitutional Revolution. In his writings, he comes off not as a politician, but rather as a Western orientalist who examines funerals, religious ceremonies, poetry, local culture, customs, and education. From his

---

143 Edmond O'Donvan, *Today's Iran*, (London, Oasis, 1882), 406-409.

144 Carla Serena, translator Golamreza Samee, *Iran's people and sights*, Mardum va dīdanīhā-yi Īrān : safar'nāmah,(Tehran, Nashre No, 1984),182-183.

145 Ibid 186-187.

146 Ibid 183-185.

reports, we obtain very precise documentation of a ten-day program of performances in the month of Muharram:[147]

1. Play about the death of Muhammad;

2. Play on the death of Fatima;[148]

3. Play migration show from Medina[149] to al Kufa;[150]

4. Death of the Muslim[151] with his two sons and report of Amir Teimur;[152]

5. Entry of Hoseyn in Kerbela and death of Al-Hurr ibn Yazid al Tamami;[153]

6. Morning: death of Abu al Fazl. Evening: Solomon's coming to help Hoseyn;

7. Morning: death of Ali Akbar.[154] In the evening: the life of Joseph;

8. Ghasem's[155] death. In the evening: Solomon's marriage to the Queen of Sheba;

9. Hoseyn's family in prison;

10. Death of Hoseyn;

---

[147] Eugene Aubin, Translator Ali Asgar Saidi, *Today's Iran*, 192.

[148] Fatima bint Muhammad (605-633) was the fourth daughter of the Prophet of Islam Muhammad.

[149] Medina, a city in Saudi Arabia.

[150] A city in Saudi Arabia.

[151] Muslim: Muslim ibn Aqil (642-680) was a friend of Hoseyn. Son of a cousin of Muhammad.

[152] Amir Timur Tamerlane (1370-1405) great Turkish-Mongol leader and general.

[153] Al -Hurr ibn Yazid al Tamami, great general of Yazid, who then went on to fight alongside Hoseyn.

[154] Ali Akbar, eldest son of Hussein, was killed in Kerbala by soldiers of Yazid ibn Mu'awiya.

[155] He was the son of Hasan ibn Ali.

Aubin thinks the best shows were held in Tekie Dowlat where admission for the public was free. At that time the English embassy contributed to the production of the Ta'ziyah and for this reason, the people, out of gratitude, celebrated the funeral in front of the embassy.[156]

Aubin also communicates to us information about a person called Moin ol Boca[157] and reports that he was an old man with white hair and a beard, carrying a wooden stick (Metrag) and rolls of parchment in his hands, and who behaved like a director and typically organized the scene, getting a lot of respect from the people. He also describes the scenography of the show, which was brilliantly simple, since all the elements of the scene were symbolic and the principal actors who played the role of the saints had pleasant voices and faces; alternatively, to perform enemies, the actors adopted unpleasant expressions and voices.[158]

In addition to the ten-day plays we discussed, Aubin recounts two other types of shows. The first one was held by amateurs, and people still went to watch it. The other one was Ta'ziyah Mozhek, which frequently attracted audiences and caused the Ta'ziyah to weaken.

In the handwritten Document [Fig 18] dated May 1905, it is explained that it was customary for the Persian people to invite the families of foreign ambassadors to attend the Ta'ziyah on one of the first ten days of the month of Muharram. This was because they knew the ambassadors' interest in and appreciation for Persian plays.

---

[156] Eugène Aubin, translator Ali Asgar Saidi, *Today's Iran* 189-190

[157] Ta'ziyah director.

[158] Eugène Aubin, translator Ali Asgar Saidi, *Today's Iran*. 192.

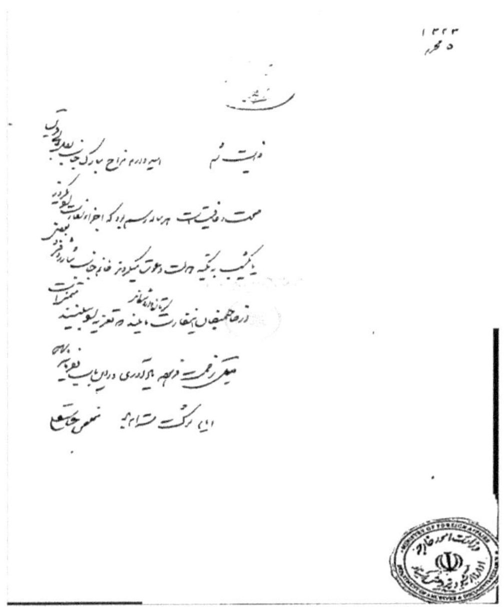

Fig 18. Handwritten document on inviting foreign ambassadors' families to Ta'ziyah performances, Muharram, Tehran, 1905. Archive of the Ministry of Foreign Affairs of Iran

Non-religious plays

The Comedy begins.

Comedy plays enjoyed a centuries-old tradition in ancient Persia. This spectacular genre originated before the establishment of Islam when spectacular forms like Mir noruzi and Kuse bar neshin were widespread. However, the most ancient documents on comedy play date back to the Safavid period. We nevertheless recognize that prior to the Safavids, there were jesters who entertained the king and governors with their comedic performances in the royal courtyards. These jesters would also venture into the squares and streets to entertain the general public. In the years since Safavid rule, Persian society had seen another type of comedy show titled Baghaal bazi,[159] which drew its inspiration from the traditional scenes of interaction between buyers and sellers in Persian markets of that period.

Naturally even after the period of the Safavids, in the age of the Qajars, there were many European travelers who for various reasons arrived in Persia and wrote travel memoirs, full of information on the religious and comic performances in use in the country, and which today we use as sources for theater history.

J.B. Fraser (1783-1856), a Scottish artist and writer who was present in Persia during the reign of Fath Ali Shah, writes:

> However the most ancient documents on comedy plays date back to the Safavid period. This show was vulgar. Afterwards, there was a

---

[159] It usually had two main players, an overly rich and stingy merchant with a lazy servant who pretended to work.
The servant was wrong in carrying out his master's orders and these mistakes created comical situations. In a Baghal bazi show there was a rich merchant and a hungry poor man who wanted to steal some yogurt from the rich man. The poor man every minute came with a different trick and tried to deceive him and, in the end, he stole the Yogurt and ran away. The rich man followed him to punish him, giving rise to a whole series of elementary but effective comic scenes, also interspersed with the performance of some ridiculous dances.
This Persian spectacular form was short-lived and usually, when presented in the villages, was performed only to make people laugh. Instead, when the performances took place in large cities or in the royal court, before the king and princes with musical intervals, the show could also contain sharp criticisms of the political situation. The actors used the various accents of the different Persian cities and tried to make brilliant improvisations, even performing parodies of the government often pleasing to the audience. There was no governmental institution capable of censoring these improvisations, so the actors over time refined the technique of improvisation on current affairs and politics.
In the Baghal bazi which was usually played in parties like Norooz and Eyde Fitr, there was no script and the actors acted improvising with the various objects they had at their disposal. If there is now a script of the Baghal bazi, it was composed after an interpretation.

> pantomime show, which was even worse than the previous one. It featured an old man with two unattractive women wearing unusual masks, resembling Pantalone. At that time, they did a show called Taghlid, which was a vulgar Punch and Judy impersonation. There were in addition four boys who danced to music while the show was going on. Their dance was so much like an Indian dance called the scorpion.[160]

Another European traveler, Gaspar Drouville, believes that there are no plays in Persia. He suggests that the performances we have described are crude jokes performed on stage, similar to a vulgar Italian comedy. In his travel memoir, he recounts, "In one scene, some crafty thieves were stealing jam and cheeses from vendors. The actors weren't professionals, but with the words and phrases they used, they improvised a comical scene for the audience. We can say that they resembled European amateur comedians."[161]

---

[160] J.B Fraser, translator Manuchehr Amiri, *Winter travel memoirs*,(Tehran, Tus, 1984), 192.

[161] Gaspar Drouvolle, translator Manuchehr Etemad Moghadam, *Voyage en Perse, atlas*, (Tehran, shabaviz, 1986) 213-14.

Fig. 19. Actors of a Taghlid company, Golestan Place, Qajar period

The author thinks a fundamental element of these comedy shows was improvisation and that the actors produced the show on a theme established by the master of the scene or party.

The Taghlid constitutes the basis of Persian comedy shows. In the Qajar period, the term "Taghlid" corresponds to Italian comedy. It was the kind of show that, whilst making people laugh, also criticized society. In fact, while carrying it out, it was possible to make observations that were not permitted in other contexts. The actors who enacted Taghlid were called Taghlidci or Moghaled (imitators). Their ability to imitate various accents from different cities created a comic situation and a discreet alienating effect which allowed for criticism of society.

Bahram Beyzaee, in his book *Spectacle in Iran*, suggests that the term "Taghlid" may have originated from the practice of imitating different accents during performances. One of their plays could include a scene in which three or four people from various cities would come; and after greeting and arguing, these people would start arguing and while arguing they created misunderstandings with their accents, then at last the story ended with a ridiculous scene.[162]

Fig. 20. Actors of taghlid, Golestan Place, Qajar period

In the Taghlid show, there was usually no set design and the spectators would sit in a circle to watch the scene. The nobles and important characters of the city were always in the front row; in the center was a high stage for the actors who, initially, recited a prologue. As soon as the audience started to get excited the actors performed pantomime actions which started the main show with music.

The actors traveled to all parts of Persia and sometimes even performed in shows with animals (monkeys and bears).

Another source of news obtains to the testimony of Carla Serena (1824-1884), an Italian traveler who went to Persia in the period of Naser al-din Shah. In her travel memoir, she wrote about the actors who made comedic shows, some of

162 Bahram Beyzaee, *Theatre in Iran*, [Namāyish dar Īrān], 169-170.

whom took salaries from the Persian government, even though they also had another job: "Usually the young and good-looking boys danced; in fact, as soon as they put on their women's clothes it was very difficult to know who was female and who was male, and the actors who played Taghlid always tried to make people laugh."[163]

Naturally, in the courts of all Persian governors, it was customary for there to be buffoons, who staged nothing but comic spectacles. These buffoons, at the moment of acting out fictional scenarios, could criticize all politicians and ruling princes without fear of punishment.

Notwithstanding the Qajar government, some of these comedians worked in the royal courts. Of comedians from that era, we have precise information about three of them. During the reign of Agha Mohammad Khan, there was a highly renowned comedian named Luti Salah. In the time of Naser al-din Shah, there were two well-known comedians named Karim Shiree and Ismail Bazzaz. These actors possessed a troupe of reciters and musicians who usually worked alongside them. One actor could play a musical instrument and sing, and some of the actors could also perform the Kakaee, a specific dance of the Persian comedy show.

Mirza Hasan Khan Tahvildar in his geography of Isfahan says that the actors were divided into two categories:[164]

1. Luti

2. Musicians

[163] Carla Serena, translator Golamreza Samee, *Iran's people and sights*, Mardum va dīdanīhā-yi Īrān : safar′nāmah, 267.
[164] Hoseyn ibn Mohamad ibn Tahvildar Isfahan, *The geography of Isfahan*, [Jughrāfiyā-yi Iṣfahān : jughrāfiyā-yi .tabīʻī va insānī va āmār-i aṣnāf-i shahr], (Tehran, Akhtaran, 2009), 87.

From this observation, we can infer that during that period, actors and musicians were highly skilled individuals who were recognized for their various abilities.

In fact, in the Qajar court, there were two offices called Luti Khane and Naghareh Khane, which were responsible for managing the actors and musicians. Each organ had a leader who was appointed by the king.

The main characters of the Taghlid were:[165]

1. The Haji, who was typically old;

2. Firuz, the servant;

3. The Haji's wife;

4. The maidservant;

5. Fokoli, a boy who dressed and behaved according to European customs.

Fig. 21. Taghlid actors with mask, Golestan Place, Qajar period

[165] Abd allah Mostofi, *Explaining of My life*, Sharḥ-i zindagānī-i man, yā, Tārīkh-i ijtimāʿī va idārī-i dawrah-i Qājārīyah , (Tehran, Zavar, 1998), 361.

Each city had a few troupes of comedians, consisting of both professional and amateur actors. Each actor had a character and consistently played the same role. Until the end of the Qajar government, young and attractive boys were cast in feminine roles instead of women.

Another person who contributed to the advancement of this spectacular art form was Moaier ol Mamalek (Nezam ol dole). He was one of those wealthy Persians who patronized a company of actors. Sometimes, he performed Naghali by himself and was well-versed in Persian plays. He also made an effort to remain abreast of the European theatre and extended invitations to foreigners and ambassadors from various countries to witness his performances. Every so often he was also involved in the Ta'ziyah, but in his own ridiculous variant of the form. Karim Shiree and Ismail Bazzaz were influenced by him and his productions.[166]

An undoubtedly unique and very singular character was Karim Shirei. He played the role of Jester at the court of Nasser al-Din Shah Qajar (1848-1896) and was originally from Isfahan. At the age of twenty, he moved to Tehran, starting a brilliant career as an itinerant actor, working on exhibitions, weddings, etc.

His fame was so great that even the king decided to summon him to the palace, as he wanted him to perform in front of him. Despite his initial fear and distrust, Karim soon showcased his qualities and his sarcasm, mocking the court's characters in front of those in power. This impudence earned him the sympathy of the king, who decided to welcome him as a court jester and a jester for the rest of his life, having obtained permission to be able to make fun of everyone

---

[166] Mayel Baktash, *Evolution of Taghlid*,(Tehranو Faslnameye Teatr, 1984), 42-43.

without suffering punishment given the direct support of the sovereign.[167]

Karim's career was undoubtedly a turning point in Persian comedy, so much so that, after him, all the artists who wanted to improvise plays used him as a point of reference.

Another legendary comedian of Naser al-din Shah's time was Ismail Bazzaz. He was born in Isfahan and moved to Tehran to work at the king's court. Bazzaz means the one who sells fabrics.[168] In fact, before becoming an actor Bazzaz had worked in a fabric shop, an activity for which he brought in collaboration with a company of comedians who went to the homes of the rich and did Taghlid shows and paid comedy shows. When Dar al Fonun's school was inaugurated with a play, he was one of the actors who performed in Molière's

Fig. 22. Company of Taghlid actors from the period of Naser al din Shah. The actor in the center of the photo is Karim Shiree, Golestan Place, Qajar period

play *Le Medécin volant*. The realization of this show required integration between the traditional ways of carrying out Persian and European theatrical productions.

167 Bahram Beyzaee, *Theatre in Iran*, [Namāyish dar Īrān], 177.
168 Mohammad Moein, *Persian dictionary*, Farhang-i Fārsī, 418.

In the last years of his life, Ismail Bazzaz stopped acting and became devoted to the precepts of religion, even constructing a mosque and with the money he had earned.

The items required by the Taghlid were found in the city. All the things that happened in the show retained a connection with society: with exaggerations and other spectacular techniques, they created a Taghlid.

A special type of Taghlid that was accepted in Persian society and became widespread was Baghal bazi. This recitation narrates the story of a stupid and very stingy head of a grocery store, with a clumsy servant, who always makes mistakes in every task he performs. Furthermore, two cunning customers want to steal something from him, and all four speak with particular accents, making ridiculous jokes.

In the Kachalak bazi (Show of a Bald Man) there is a bald slacker, jobless, who loves a beautiful and rich girl, and he always goes to her house in hopes of marrying her, which does not happen because her father does not accept him. The bald man could on occasion fight against an ogre or some generic enemies to save the girl, usually a princess.

Ultimately we can divide Taghlid into four main types:

• Taghlid on historical and mythological subjects;

• Taghlid dealing with current affairs;

• Fantasy Taghlids;

• Immoral Taghlids.

Fig. 23. The Musicians group of Taghlid, Golestan Place, Qajar period

As we have explained, Taghlid was the evolution of the short recitations that solo actors and small groups of performers made in the king's courts. By integrating dances, songs, pantomimes and dialogues, the transformation of this kind of entertainment was achieved.

In the Taghlid there was no scenography. The stage was a platform that the actors stepped onto when they wanted to perform. The actors also wore no special costumes, only rarely wore make-up, and sometimes applied false cotton beards.

Fig: 24. The Musicians and Dancer group, Golestan Place, Qajar period

The show began with music and continued with an interlude, usually a dialogue between two actors. After the intermezzo the second act began, and at the end of the performances, there was music again.

These performances could take place in cafes and tearooms or outdoors in public squares. Before the show, the artists toured the city and played and sang to invite the population. Famous groups of actors sometimes even had a few servants to carry their bags. The actors performing the dance usually used masks; however, it was the women who wore makeup. The important musical instruments were the tar, tonbak, kamancheh, and dayereh.

We can say that the Taghlid was a Persian private performance of the Qajar period, which was sometimes performed by women. We do not have much information about female Taghlid, but we can say that it was a theatrical genre inspired by different conventional situations of Persian society.

Performances by women took place behind closed doors, and male audiences were not allowed to attend the performances. When a male character was required, a woman dressed as a man and acted for him. Usually, the shows were staged in a room of the house of a famous or political, or wealthy person.

Play of clowns

Buffoons, in Persian, can have different names, such as Dalgak, Talkhak, or Maskhare:[169] if we consider the last term (Maskhare) we immediately notice the similarity with the Italian *maschera*.[170]

The history of clowns (known as Dalgak, Talkhak, or Maskhare in Persian) dates back to the Achaemenid period, predating the rise of Islam. Some of these clowns donned the mask. In the war between Persia and Rome in 53 BC., the Persians killed an important Roman figure, Marcus Licinius Crassus. The Persians were led by a famous captain named Surena. At the end of the war, the Persian soldiers discovered a soldier who closely resembled Crassus. They compelled him to wear women's clothing and paraded him around the city as a means of humiliating the Roman enemy. This spectacular form was later reproduced before the king.

Most of the information in our possession comes after the affirmation of Islam when in the courts of the king the solo actors made performances of buffoons. Some kings had clowns who worked only for them and were allowed to say anything they wished.[171]

---

169 Mohammad Moein, *Persian dictionary*, Farhang-i Fārsī, 1103.

170 Mask.

171 In the history of Iran, most of the kings had clowns in their courts, but unfortunately, due to various reasons, including resentment towards theatre, especially comedy, today we have less information about them.

Clowns were usually present at royal court parties as guests of the king and, therefore, when the king paid a jester, he was authorized to say and do whatever he pleased. A buffoon had to know how to dance and sing, and it was especially appreciated if he could act improvised.

After the Safavid period, clowns performed in cities such as Isfahan, in public places—for example, in cafes. When Tehran became the capital, many clowns moved there to work.

Fig. 25. Two clowns, Golestan Place, Golestan Place, Qajar period.

Azod al Doleh, in his book on the history of Azdi, mentions a clown known as Loti Saleh. The clown had a lot of money, and Agha Mohammad Khan, as soon as he realizes this, tries to take his money. The fool replies: "God has not given you a donation, take my money but don't bother my body." Agha Mohammad Khan retorts, "I have to treat you differently. So you can't go to the party to make people laugh." Then the king orders to cut off the fool's nose.

We can mention as Talhak, who was the court clown of Sultan Mahmud Ghaznavi, Kal Enayat I the clown of the court of Shah Abbas or Haj Mirza Zakikhan the clown of the court of Ahmad Shah Qajar.

After the cutting off of the nose, the jester says: "You understand that god has not given you the donation." As soon as the king hears this sentence, he orders him to give back his money and says: "Go and pray, I'm afraid you'll get angry."[172]

It is very well understood that the period of the reign of Agha Mohammad Khan was not very favorable for clowns, because, as mentioned, the ruler was engaged in continuous wars.

Fig. 26. Karim Shiree and Abbas Geda two actors of taghlid, Golestan Place, Qajar period

Carla Serena, the renowned Italian traveler, asserts that Persian buffoons bear resemblance to European clowns who were employed in circuses. She further explains that clowns received a salary from the government while also pursuing other occupations; in fact they usually performed shows in front of the king and his women.[173]

Another traveler, Gaspar Drovil, says that improvisation is a fundamental motif in the acting of clowns and believes that

---

172 Azod ol doleh, *History of Azodi*, Tārīkh-i 'Azụdī, 165-166.
173 Carla Serena, translator Golamreza Samee, *Iran's people and sights*, [Mardum va dīdanīhā-yi Īrān : safar'nāmah], 267.

Persian and Italian buffoons are very similar. Over time the buffoons moved away from the courts and collaborated with the theater companies of the Takhte hozi.[174]

Takhte Hozi

As we have discussed, the name Takhte Hozi integrates two words, which mean "wood" and "fountain." In fact, the period from the last years of the Safavid government to the end of the Qajar era was a particularly rich period for Persian comedy shows, as solo actors began to gather into a company and work in groups.

During the Qajar period,[175] this type of show took place in most of the cities of Persia and offered an additional occasion for the actors to enter the king's court. At every party there were always actors who made the princes laugh. Usually, in such shows there was a critique of the contemporary social situation, which was allowed the actors only in the moment of stage fiction. Subsequently, this show also entered the homes of nobles, on the occasion of wedding parties or other parties in private homes at the invitation of the landlord. If a company had a famous actor who also worked in the royal court, that company was highly regarded. In the Qajar period such performances also took place in public places, such as coffee houses.

In the Takhte Hozi there are two main and fundamental characters: the servant, *Siah*, and the old man, *Arbab*.

Arbab (Haji Posh) is the boss of Siah, and takes on the main character of the old man, a miserly person who represents the bourgeois class. Other types of characters also appear in this form of entertainment, like lovers. Usually, it was a young

---

174 Gaspar Drouvolle, translator Manuchehr Etemad Moghadam, *Voyage en Perse, atlas*, 213-214.

175 They reigned in Persia from 1794 to 1925.

boy in love with a very wealthy or very poor girl. If the boy was rich, then the girl was from a disadvantaged but noble family, whereas if the boy was poor, the girl was the daughter of a king or a rich man.[176]

Fig. 28. Example for Takhte hozi, Florence, Italy.

When women could not participate in the performances in front of males, usually a young boy acted in place of the women. Sometimes when the scene was not serious, a very ridiculous and comical situation would happen between the actor playing in the woman's place and the other actor.

Another important character in this show remains the minister who played the role of antagonist and usually opposed the actions of Siah.

In some of the fantastic genre texts, there was also a magician, who was usually a negative character in the story. There was further still a minister, who was an opponent of Siah and in love.[177]

---

[176] Morteza Ahmadi, *Kohne haye hamishe no*, [Kuhnahā-i hamīšā nau : tarānahā-i taẖt-i ḥauḍī ; wīrāst-i duwwum], (Tehran, Quqnūs,2001), 199.
[177] Ibid 202.

Soldiers of the royal courts could sporadically carry out a minor role. If necessary, they could also exchange clothes and depict the characters of the people.

The music in this show was a brilliantly entertaining element, as the lead actor usually performed traditional music that people knew very well. Before introducing the show, the musicians prepared the audience by attracting their attention through the playing of instrumental pieces. As soon as there was a change of scenery on stage, the music filled this empty space and gave the actors enough time for this change.[178]

Sometimes, when the actors wanted to give information about the diverse scenic settings, they used music to evoke different atmospheres.

Equally essential, and in addition to the music, were the dances specially designed for the Takhte Hozi. Some actors performed particular and characterizing dances: for example, for example the bakers' dances, the Kakaee dance, etc.

In this type of show, there are two types of languages, both used in the different scenes to distinguish the characters of high-class extraction from the poor and humble. The king, the ministers, and the princes speak the noble language; the servant Siah and the common people speak the standard language and do not comprehend the language of the nobles, so comic scenes based on this incommunicability follow one another.

In the Takhte Hozi, the use of noble language must be considered as a habit of the influential classes, who hide their grand designs behind a false culture. The servants, aware of this use by their superiors, appropriate that sophisticated vocabulary to make fun of them.

---

178 Yaghub Azhand, *Theatre of the Qajars*, (Namāyish dar dawrah-i Qājār), 283.

We can say the presentation of this type of show in the various cities with various accents created a spectacular comic situation and, through the addition of modern words, a spectacular language typical of Takhte Hozi was established.

Takhte Hozi can be divided into four chief types:

• Historical-mythological Takhte Hozi, related to ancient history and Persian mythology;

• The current affairs Takhte Hozi;

• The Takhte Hozi inspired by fictional subjects;

• The satirical or vulgar Takhte Hozi.

The topics covered in this show are extremely fascinating; in fact, they all come from the heart of the society of the time and especially from the poor people who formed the majority of the city's inhabitants.

This play employs some spectacular techniques aimed at making the audience laugh. A second critical technique involves inserting proverbs with comic variations. When in a scene the actor repeats a sentence five times with slight nuances of meaning, or, during the performance, when an actor rehearses the words that his partner has said, making the latter nervous, comedic situations arise.

A second critical technique involves inserting proverbs with comic variations. An actor thus proposes a famous proverb, which everyone knows, but his partner changes this motto into a comic form.

Another important technique is the interruption of the speeches of the one who is about to speak: the actor, while he wants to say something important, is interrupted by his partner as soon as he begins speaking.

The puppet plays

The actor, while he wants to say something important, is interrupted by his partner as soon as he begins speaking. In fact, even in those regional cultures, various puppet shows resemble the Persian puppet show. But the forms and the stories and the characters that are in the Persian puppet show have a properly local basis. In fact, some of these characters are found in books like the *Shahnameh*.

The puppets of this type of show represent real characters: among the most popular is Pahlevan Kachal, or the bald champion.

There are two theories on the origin of this figure: the first affirms the existence of a master of this spectacular form, who was, in fact, hairless. The second, however, claims that Pahlevan kachal is actually a mythological character, who became famous due to the many wars he fought.[179]

Tahvildari, in his book on the geography of Isfahan, talks about these shows and thinks that the actors who made these shows were the Luti who, on festive nights, went to the main squares and created a paper and fabric structure with which they made representations with various colors and various[180] voices. From Tahvildar's writings we understand how this play was made in Isfahan, and then was later transferred to Tehran.

The great Persian writer Etemad ol Saltaneh in his book *Ruznameye khaterat* writes: "Tonight they did Hoghe bazi (puppet Plays) again [...]." He invited actors who did puppet

[179] Bahram Beyzaee, *Theatre in Iran*, [Namāyish dar Īrān], 99.
[180] Hoseyn ibn Mohamad ibn Tahvildar Isfahan, *The geography of Isfahan*, [Jughrāfiyā-yi Iṣfahān : jughrāfiyā-yi .tabī'ī va insānī va āmār-i aṣnāf-i shahr], 86.

shows to his house and paid them because he wanted his family to watch the plays too.[181]

Alexander Chodzko,[182] in his book on Iranian theatre says the puppet show is a national show for the Persians, especially in the parts that speak Azeri [...].[183] "The characters in the show love all the beautiful things in the world [...]. You eat well, you drink well, you live well, and you are always happy."[184]

There were two main types of puppet shows in Persia, but before explaining these two forms we need to introduce two actors with two different names: Ostad (master), who made the puppets move, and Morshed, who was next to the puppets and usually played a musical instrument called tonbak; when the voice of the actors was not clear, he explained everything.

1. Kheyme shab bazi (Marionette)

This type of play was produced with two variations: in the first form there was a big old chest that opened towards the spectators and the master hid behind the chest and made the puppets move with a string. To the right and left of the case obtain two lights.

In the second form, which typically took place in a room, a curtain was placed on the wall and the master sat behind the curtain only letting his hands come out. The puppets were like gloves and the master played with the dolls and in his mouth he had a small wind instrument (called safir), the end of which was placed behind the lower teeth. He thus

181 Mohamad Hasan Khan Etemad ol saltaneh, *Journal of Memories*, [Khāṭirāt-i I'timād al-Salṭanah], 646

182 (1804 –1891) was a Polish orientalist.

183 Mohamad Hasan Khan Etemad ol saltaneh, *Journal of Memories*, [Khāṭirāt-i I'timād al-Salṭanah],425.

184 Aleksandro Chodzko, translator Jalal Satari, *The Persian theater*, 15-19.

produced a whistle that when he spoke imparted a particular color to the dialogues.

Sometimes, there were also two people who accompanied the show with musical instruments: the kamancheh and the tonbak. Ostad and Morshed were the ones in charge of organizing the show, including narration and development.

2. *Saye Bazi (shadow play)*

There was a curtain in front of which a great light was placed. When the puppets behind the curtain began to move, the shadow on the curtain amplified all their gestures. This form of acting was usually used for fictional stories.

There were five main characters in this form of entertainment:[185]

1) Pahlevan Kachal (the bald champion);

2) Akhond (Mullah);

3) Bibi (an old woman);

4) Rostam (a very strong man, like Hercules);

5) The ogre.

When more secondary characters were needed, they were added from time to time.

One of the most famous subjects of puppet shows of the Qajar period is "Sultan Salim's[186] court. Some scholars think this title dates back to the Safavid period when the Chaldran War was going on between the Persians and the Ottomans. The king of the Ottomans at that time was Sultan Salim:

185 Bahram Beyzaee, *Theatre in Iran*, [Namāyish dar Īrān], 100.

186 (1465 –1520) was Sultan of the Ottoman Empire from 1512 to his death.

scholars think this spectacular story was born to joke with Sultan Salim. Sixty-six puppets participated in the Sultan Salim show. But the story was very simple.[187]

Another very pleasant subject began with the Morshed, relating a poem by a great famous Persian poet named Hafez. The poem spoke of the unity of the god, then some puppets came out and said the king was entering; others cleaned the road and called the people to come as the king passed. The king entered, the musicians played, others danced and the buffoons put on the play.

A person called "Luti" told the king that his salary is not enough and asked for more and the king, Morshed, replied that the king had given him money and asked what he had done with it. Luti replied that one of his vezir had taken everything from him and that he was left with nothing. At one point the king called the ogre who came to punish the Vezir.[188]

In another story, the bald champion loved a girl called Golrokh, but his father didn't give him permission to get married. At one point there was a servant called Firuz who helped the champion to get to the girl. The show ended with the marriage between the two young people.[189] The character of Pahlevan Kachal can be likened to the Turkish Karagöz.

The other kind of Plays

When there are so many languages, cultures, and customs in a country, practically in every corner of a city, you can witness

---

[187] Yaghub Azhand, *Theatre of the Qajars*,(Namāyish dar dawrah-i Qājār), 294-295.

[188] Bahram Beyzaee, *Theatre in Iran*, [Namāyish dar Īrān], 96-97.

[189] Jafar Shahri, *Social history of Teherean in the 13th century*, [Tārīkh-i ijtimāʻī-i Tihrān dar qarn-i sīzdahum : zindagī, kasb va kār],(Tehran, Yasa va Esmailian, 1389), 37.

various performances that reflect a shared experience. Indeed, to mark the arrival of spring, the different shows symbolically celebrated the cyclical rebirth of the year.

Another very important aspect was the Persian calendar. In ancient Persia, each year had two seasons and twelve months, with each month consisting of thirty days. Thus, in a Persian year, there were five extra days known as "stolen palms" that fell within the last five days of winter. In reality, the Persian New Year marks the first day of spring. During this period, the population engaged in public activities such as whitewashing or cleaning city buildings.

As we have explained, during the last five days of the Persian year, many events and performances were held to celebrate the arrival of spring. The most important spectacle that originated in the Achaemenid period is Kuse bar shin, which spread to various cities. One such performance that falls under this category is Tulki zani (fox beating), an ancient ritual that existed during the Qajar period and later transformed into a show similar to Tulki zani. As we have explained, during the last five days of the Persian year, numerous shows were held to celebrate the arrival of spring. These actors would go to places such as coffee houses or occasionally perform in the main squares of cities. When the singer-storyteller sang, the wolf danced and slowly the dog came. As soon as the wolf saw the dog, he played dead. At one point the singer would take gifts or money from people. They routinely did this show in northeastern Persia, in regions where Azeri was spoken.

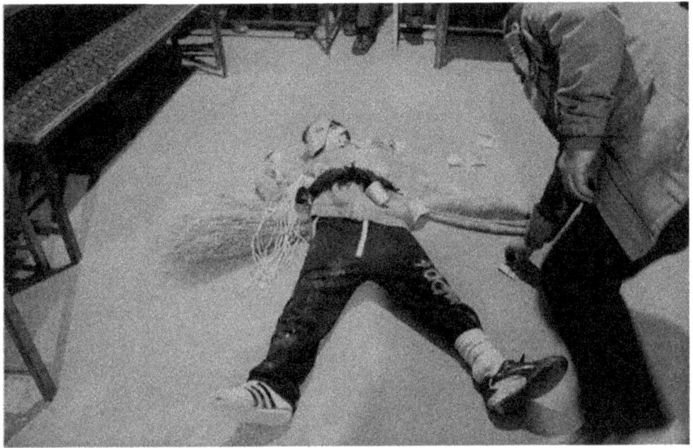

Fig. 29. An example for Tulki Zani kind of Persian theatrical performance, Jolfa, the picture took by author in 2018.

On the last five days of the year, all the elders of the city used to go to the house of one of the local noblemen to take part in a performance entitled Charshanba Nana (Grandmother on Wednesday). Before starting, the master of the house offered food and sweets to all the guests.

An elderly woman who was chosen by the people performed this show: first, she chose a wall and cleaned it thoroughly, then she brought flour and water; the woman wet her hands and with her fingers took a little flour to put on the wall to make particular drawings of primitive form. She used to draw a person, the sun, and all those things that one wishes for in the New Year. Finally, instead of the person's mouth, they put a grape raisin that was supposed to bring good luck.

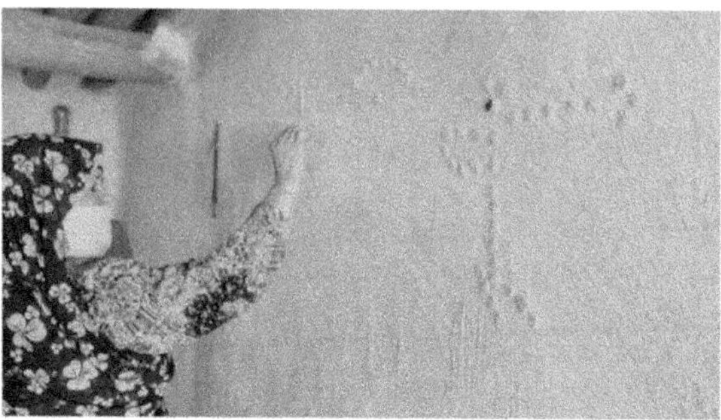

Fig. 30. Grandmother on Wednesday, Jolfa, the picture took by author in 2018.

Another show of ancient origin, which was usually performed on religious festivals, especially in remembrance of the death of a saint, was the Sham garden, which means to spin the candle. Documents [...] and [...] date back to the last years of the Qajar government and discuss a show made together with other religious shows such as the Roze Khani or Ta'ziyah o nohe Khani. The show was performed in the city of Mashhad at the Harem of Imam Reza: people carried the candle and walked around the Harem, with one person performing Rozeh while walking.

During the Qajar period, a category of the show called Mareke was very important which brought together jugglers, animal games, wrestling, and tightrope walking. As the acclaimed Persian writer Jamalzadeh[190] recalls, Mareke consists of gathering people together and performing shows such as juggling exhibitions, animal games, fights, tightrope walking, and games with snakes: ultimately, money was

---

[190] Mohamad Ali Jamalzadeh (1892- November 8, 1997), was one of the most important writers of Persia in the 20th century.

requested. The people who behind this show are Mareke Gir.[191]

In the Qajar period, all the plays came from previous periods, and they underwent modifications over time.

Tahvildar, in his geography of Isfahan, claims that all the actors who played Marake were called Luti.[192]

There were seven types of Luti:

1. Musicians and animal trainers;

2. Tightrope walkers;

3. Puppeteers;

4. Baghal bazi performers;

5. Zodiac performers and jugglers;

6. Lion trainers;

7. Drunks, thieves, and gamblers.

One of these Luti, when he found the genuine place, made his show of him. Other Luti traveled, and when they found a good enough place in a city or a small town they put on their play.[193]

James Morier, English politician and writer, on his journey to Persia, saw the spectacles of the king's court and in his travel memoirs he writes:

---

191 Mohammad Ali Jamalzadeh, *Folk vocabulary*, [Farhang-i lughāt-i 'āmiyānah], (Tehran, Abu Sina, 1862), 402.

192 Hoseyn ibn Mohamad ibn Tahvildar Isfahan, *The geography of Isfahan*, [Jughrāfiyā-yi Iṣfahān: jughrāfiyā-yi .tabī'ī va insānī va āmār-i aṣnāf-i shahr], 86-87.

193 Abd allah Mostofi, *Explaining of My life*, Sharḥ-i zindagānī-i man, yā, Tārīkh-i ijtimā'ī va idārī-i dawrah-i Qājārīyah, 304.

> The tightrope walkers were extremely excellent. After this show, they brought an elephant. The elephant before the king sat and howled, so he greeted the king. Afterward, there were the others who wrestled [...]. The king rewarded the winners with money.[194]

Carla Serena, the Italian traveler who was in Persia during the period of Naser Al-Din Shah, remarks:

> For the Persian New Year, the actors who played Mareke came to the king's court. The government paid all the actors. These actors usually have other jobs and only play during holidays.[195]

Jakob Eduard Polak, a German doctor who lived in Persia for quite a long time and who saw many of Mareke's performances, recalls that "The king from behind the window of his court watched the show and divided the money and gifts among the actors. Those who wrestled were half-naked and had no shirt on. Other comedians wore loincloth or tiger skins [...]. Other actors performed shows with animals [...]."[196]

---

[194] James Morier, translator Abolghasem Seri, *Travel memoirs* 193.

[195] Carla Serena, translator Golamreza Samee, *Iran's people and sights*, [Mardum va dīdanīhā-yi Īrān : safar'nāmah], 267.

[196] Jakob Eduard Polak, translator Keikavus Jahandari, *Iran and Iranian*, [Safarnāmah-i Pūlāk : Irān va Irāniyān] (Tehran, Kharazmi, 1983), 262.

Fig. 31.Example for theatrical performance of Mareke, Golestan Place, Qajar period.

Instead, James Morier saw a man eating fire:

"There was a big pot of fire and a man would take a piece and put it in his mouth and put it out."[197]

Persian society had achieved the political and cultural potential necessary to implement significant reforms across all levels and aspects of Qajar society. Society is still divided into two parts: the religious and conservative group who adhere to the traditional ways of their ancestors, and the intellectuals who often have had the opportunity to gain experiences abroad, particularly for educational purposes. When these gifted students returned home, especially from Russia and France, they brought back a modern culture.

In the final years of the Qajar government and immediately following the Persian Constitutional Revolution, one of the pioneering companies in Tehran was the Farhang (Culture)

---

[197] James Morier, translator Abolghasem Seri, *Travel memoirs*, 244.

Company. It was established in Atabak Park, which was located in a highly sophisticated area. The founders of the company were Mohamad Ali Forughi and Abdolah Mostofi. Belatedly, for their gatherings, they selected Masudieh Palace, which was in close proximity to the Persian Parliament. The Farhang Company (1907-1909) was involved in promoting culture through the world of theatre and producing shows that were accessible to the public free of charge. "There was a large bonfire, and a man would take a piece of it and place it in his mouth, extinguishing it." After this company, another private company called the Theatre Melli (National Theatre) established itself and was active from 1909 to 1915 when it was forced to close due to political problems. When these students returned home, especially from Russia and France, they imported a modern culture. One of the first foreign operas staged in this theater was *The Inspector General* by the Russian writer Nikolai Gogol. The capacity of this musical theater was not high and only fifty spectators could go there. In its six operational years of life, the theatre produced twenty different shows, including several works by Molière.

There were also other groups interested in promoting culture in Persia. Musical comedy was taken care of by representatives such as Mirzade Eshgi, Abol Ghasem Lahuti and Hasan Moghadam, or associations such as the Musical Club, whose head was Ali naghi vasiri, and finally the Kanune Iran Javan, headed by Reza Kamal Shahrzad. There were also theatre groups of other societies and religions, such as those of the Armenians and the Zoroastrians, whose Persian theatre troupe began to operate in the last years of the Qajar government.

Another significant city for the production of modern plays was Tabriz, which borders countries close to Russia. The road that passed through Tabriz and reached the capital became the creator of spectacular communication and integration opportunities, so much so that in the Qajar period many Persian students from Tabriz went to Russia to continue studying. The subsequent Persian constitutional revolution saw as most of its architects precisely the intellectuals who had studied abroad.

In addition to the Russian influences on the Persian theater in Tabriz, in the Qajar period, there were, in addition, those of the Ottomans, who, for centuries, had good relations with the population of Tabriz—thanks to the similarity of the two languages. The Ottomans who were close to Europe had assimilated the present form of European theater and precisely because of their relations with Tabriz they probably passed on their influence to the theatre of the Persian city.[198]

It is worth recalling that the Armenian society inevitably made shows for local consumption; practically they had adopted a new science imported from abroad to Persia. Indeed, in 1881, just around the time of Naser al-din Shah's reign, Mr. Safaratian entered Persia from Russia and produced a play called *Othello*. The first show that the Armenians had done dates back to 1879 and was organized by Mesrop Papasian in his house. So we can say that in Tabriz there were two main channels for theatrical importation.[199]

---

198 Amir Alizadegan, *History of the Theater of Tabriz*, (Tehran Faslnameye teatr, 1988), 75-76.
199 Gilbert Moshk Anbarians, *A look at Armenian theater in Iran*,(Tehranو Faslnameye Peyman, 2005), n: 38, 51-52.

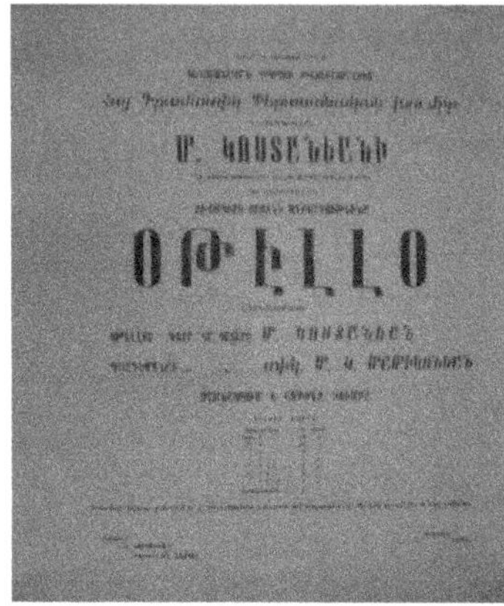

Fig. 32. Othello theatrical performance, Archive of Vank Museum, Isfahan, 1924.

The city of Rasht was near Tabriz and, basically, when theater companies came to Tabriz they also passed by Rasht and put on performances there. While the foreign groups passed by, the Armenians also made their shows. During the reign of Mohamad Ali Shah, the scholar Mirza Hasan Khan taught French in his school and translated some of Molière's plays, which were performed in Rasht. Female characters were routinely depicted by males. The first theater company in Rasht was that of Omid Torghi founded in the last years of the Qajar period. To advance culture in the Gilan region, morality shows were performed. The Farhang Society Theatre Troupe has had a positive influence on the Rasht theatre. In Russia, a very important person who worked for the theatre culture of Rasht was Mirza Hasan Khan Nemayeshi (Agha Daee).[200]

Surely another avenue for theatrical importation into Persia was Isfahan, or better put, the society of the Armenians. Since the Safavid period, and following the massive

---

[200] Basil Nikitin, translator Ali Frah vashi, *The Iran I Know*, (Tehran Marefat, 1977), 127-128.

immigration of Armenians from Yerevan to Isfahan by order of the Shah of Persia, Armenians had created their own society. In this society, exports and imports gradually increased thanks to Armenian merchants, who also spread dramatic texts during their trips.

In 1886 the Armenians founded a theater company that produced plays of European form but in Armenian and Persian languages. To found this company, the group asked for contributions from the people and so they raised 551 Geran, with which they set up the theater and financially supported the company. In 1899, another company called the Society of Theater Lovers was founded. They were very precise and official; in fact, they wrote a letter of intent with their rules. The texts translated by the Armenians were typically the European works of Molière, Shakespeare, and Schiller.[201]

The first of their theatre documents dates back to February 9, 1887, and it is a handwritten flyer of a successful show called Fico di Khecho which was made with Armenian actors. It was a musical comedy show with seven actors.

Mashhad has been for many years a destination city of pilgrimage by Muslims. In the Qajar period usually Russian and Kafkaz actors went to Mashhad for their performances. In the last years of the Qajar period, Colonel Pesian,[202] with the contribution of others, founded a fixed hall in the national garden of Mashhad, where usually the theatre groups that went there had the opportunity to perform their shows in the Azeri language.[203]

---

[201] Gilbert Moshk Anbarians, *A look at Armenian theater in Iran*, 33.

[202] Mohammad Taqi Pessian, (1892 - 1921), Persian nationalist soldier and politician.

[203] Mohamad Reza Zamani Zavarzadeh, *Theatre in Mash had*,(Tehran Faslnameye teatr, 1988), 166-167.

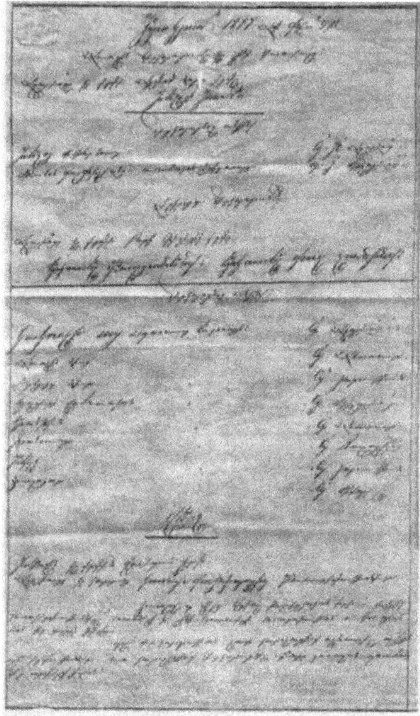

Fig. 33. Handwritten flyer for a show called Khecho's Fig.
www.abcarians.com

We have observed that during the Qajar period, apart from Tehran, there were several cities that had a multitude of theaters and the participation of foreign artists. All of these combinations that took place during the Qajar period gave rise to a new and spectacular form of Persian theater. In fact, the Qajar period marked a period of significant progress in the history of Persian theater.

CHAPTER 3:

TOWARDS MODERNIZATION OF THEATRE

After the Safavids, who attempted to unify Persia through religion, the Qajarids emerged as the second dynasty, seeking to unite the Persian people by establishing their identity. However, the country faced invasions from the Afghans, Russians, and Ottomans.

Thanks to the Afsharid dynasty, particularly through the efforts of Nader Shah, Persia successfully addressed numerous challenges related to external enemy attacks. However, the Zand dynasty soon arrived on the scne, considering themselves the only clan worthy of governing Persia after the Safavids. Society needed stability and tranquility, and after a bloody internal war that affected various regions of Persia, Agha Mohamad Khan founded the Qajar dynasty.

Most of the people were illiterate, and there was a need to import knowledge of the new sciences due to the arrival of European teachers. The communication between Persia and other countries was precisely due to the need to modernize the country and transition from a traditional and closed society to the progress of the modern world. In fact, while Persia had a rich culture and a long history, it was nevertheless very isolated and technologically behind compared to other countries of its time. The lack of relations with European society, as well as with other countries, due to religious reasons, was the main cause of the lack of progress in Persian society. Indeed, the people believed that beyond the borders of Persia, everyone was an enemy, particularly non-Muslims.

With the Constitutional Revolution, the power of the kings diminished, and the first Persian parliament was established. Communications with Europe influenced many changes, but initially, the fundamental local habits and traditions remained unchanged. Later, traditional society managed to overcome the initial resistance and began to evolve into a culturally integrated one.

The religious were opposed to the government and enjoyed the favor of the majority of the population, who believed that the only path to eternal salvation after death was through obedience to the religious precepts of Islam.

Art, especially the production of handicrafts, was not considered very important to the kings, who were not inclined to support artists. However, the abundance of imported goods necessary for the population enabled a problem-free life, even for artists.

Usually, the feudal lords had the power to do whatever they wanted. They had soldiers and weapons at their disposal. However, the population was accustomed to religious beliefs. Workers paid taxes, while merchants paid little. In each city there was a representative of the other merchants who was in charge of maintaining contact with the government. The social, political and cultural conditions of Iran at that time demanded a big change, a change that needed time to be accepted among people. These changes started with Abbas Mirza,[204] the crown prince of Fath Ali Shah,[205] and continued during the presidency of Amir Kabir,[206] reaching the ministry of Mirza Hossein Khan Sepahsalar.[207]

---

204 (1789 –1833), He was a Qajar crown prince of Iran.

205 (1769 –1834), He was the second king of Qajar Iran.

206 (1807 –1852), He was chief minister to Naser al-Din Shah Qajar.

207 (1828–1881), He was the prime minister of Iran during the Qajar Period under King Naser al-Din Shah Qajar between 1871 and 1873.

With the travels of the kings of Persia to Europe, there was a significant exchange of information regarding different lifestyles and practices. This exchange allowed for numerous updates in Persia from a Western perspective.

In the history of Persia, the Qajar period was very important as it marked the transition from a traditional society to a more modern one. This period was characterized by a relative period of peace and tranquility after numerous periods of warfare. Thanks to the reign of Naser al-Din Shah, the taboo that officially prevented Persians from traveling to non-Muslim countries was broken. Before Naser al-Din Shah, no king had ever traveled to Europe or Christian countries. In fact, during the Safavid period, there were various forms of communication between Persia and European countries. However, no one had ever made these trips until the kings of Persia in the Qajar period began to do so. From that moment many other travelers moved to Europe, bringing back home the innovations that gradually influenced Persian culture and society.

The reasons for these journeys were very diverse and ranged from economic, mercantile and political to cultural, scientific, educational, and so on. The results were revolutionary in a country that until then had closed itself to the rest of the world, especially in the entertainment sector, which even radically changed people's lives.

1. *The travels of Naser al-din Shah*[208]

As mentioned earlier, one of the great travelers of the Qajar period was Naser al din Shah, who made three trips to Europe between 1873 and 1889, during which he gained very

---

[208] The documents used in this chapter from the trips of Qajar kings to Europe have all been found by me and I have personally found them in the archives of European cities.

strong impressions and brought his Western experiences to his country. His first trip began on April 19, 1873 and took him to Germany, Belgium, England, France, Switzerland, Italy and finally to the Ottoman Empire.

The second journey of Naser al din Shah with his court began in 1878 and touched Eastern European countries such as Armenia, Georgia, Russia, Hungary and then Germany, France and Austria again.

Some of his companions were later to play a very important role: his personal "buffoon," Etemad ol Saltaneh, Naser ol molk and Prime Minister Mehdi gholi Khan knew Persian theatre well and probably paid close attention to the European performances they attended. Mehdi gholi Khan knew some European languages and was a musician who was fond of classical music. Naser al molk had studied at Oxford, knew some European languages and had translated some of Shakespeare's works.

Fig. 34. Mohammad Hasan Khan Etemad ol Saltaneh and Gholam Ali Khan Aziz al-Soltan (Malijak II), during Naser al-Din Shah's third journey to Europe, Paris, 1889. Royal Library of Paris

The Shah of Iran, who was very fond of art, used all opportunities to attend theatrical and musical performances. Apart from the interest and passion he had for seeing western art, in his writings he gives us very useful information about the form and shape of Russian theatres, which are very important. By carefully looking at his notes, you can understand his ability to recognize and distinguish between various theater performances.

Naser al-Din Shah's first continuous European tour took place in April 1873 with an eighty-four-member delegation to Russia, Germany, Belgium, England, France, Switzerland, Italy, and Austria. Apart from exploring the workings of these societies and signing political treaties, the most valuable aspect of this trip was attending operas, dances, and festivals of fireworks.

This had a great impact on the mind and soul of Shah Qajar, stimulating his refined taste and making him interested in the performance of artistic works. This was the starting point for the emergence of the photographer Naser ad-Din Shah. The Shah, who had learned the art of photography and was very interested in it, tried at every opportunity to photograph the landscape and the people around him, even Prince Malik Qasim Mirza (1843-1921). Thus, it can be said that the first

Fig. 35. Naser al-Din Shah Qajar and Emperor Franz Joseph I at the Vienna World Exhibition, 1873. Oil on canvas, 24 × 35 cm. Reproduced from Fatemeh Ghaziha.

signs of the introduction of the art of photography and later cinema and the growth of other visual arts became visible with the journey of Shah Qajar, which naturally affected the development of the art of performance and the allocation of time and space. The eventual construction of the first hotel in the new style, the establishment of the zoo and even the popularization of the lace skirts of ballet dancers as ugly household clothes for women, are considered among the achievements of this trip. The second journey of the Shah, which started in 1878 from the Caucasus, continued along the route of Russia towards Europe to Poland, Germany, Austria and France. The third and last trip of the Shah took place in 1889 to Russia, France, England, Belgium, Austria and the Ottoman lands, and if it was not for the assassination of Naser ad-Din Shah in 1896, maybe a fourth trip would have happened! But what is reflected in these travels is the recording of the Shah's personal observations from his own words or pen, which show the Shah of Iran's enthusiasm and admiration for observing the progress of Western civilization and the way of life and entertainment of Westerners. In these travel memories, the narrations are purely from his personal point of view and some of the events are either not understood correctly or have been narrated in an incomplete manner. But what is certain is that Naser ad-Din Shah, as the first king of Iran who stepped into Christian lands, obtains a great contribution in transferring the art of theatre to the country. He was somewhat influenced by Iranian art and was inclined towards painting and music. In addition to meeting with artists, he tried constructing a building for the performance of native performing arts in Tehran.

In his observations in one place, he compares the actors of one theater with another theater. Or, as in another place, an actor is compares with French actors and Karim Shiree.

Here we mention some examples of the Shah's own observations. Russia, which was one of Iran's allies at that time, was the first country that the Shah of Iran entered with other Qajar nobles at the beginning of his adventure.

Russia 1873,[209]

Astrakhan, May 14, Wednesday.

We reached a part of the theatre called the Lodge [...] it is a small theatre. There was a large crowd of men and women below [...] the theatre curtain were raised. Suddenly something strange was seen. Dance of Gods, Sky, There were three acts—that is, the curtain was lowered three times, and every time it was lowered, we went out. The weather outside was better and cooler [...].[210]

Moscow, May19, Monday.

We went up the stairs of the theatre and reached the lodge, which is located right in front of the San. The San is where the actors perform. Many people were sitting down on the chairs. The curtain was raised. A strange world was found [...] women dancers [...] one by one. Two, two, four, four, one hundred danced. This dance and performance is called ballet. It means speechless dancing [and it] is like a dumb game. They both dance and act. There are many musicians in front of the people under the dance and acting place.

---

[209] In the Russian travel section of the Naser al din Shah, I used Russian documents taken from the newspaper of Golos. The interesting thing about this newspaper was its date, which was 12 days earlier than Shah's report. The reason for this difference was the use of the Julian calendar by Rus newspaper.

[210] Naser al din shah, Edited by Majid Abd Amin, *Diary of Naser al-Din Shah Qajar the first trip in Europe*, [Rūznāmah-'i khāṭirāt-i Nāṣir al-Dīn Shāh Qājār : az Shavvāl-i 1288 tā Z̲īḥijjah-i 1290], (Tehran, Dr, Mahmud Afshar, 2020), P 201

> They play continuously. But everyone plays the fiddle. It is very nice that the dancers dance to the music of these instruments. When one act ends, the curtains fall, people rest for fifteen minutes, the curtains are raised again and another act is performed [...]. After the first act, we went to another lodge, which was close to the stage, from where it can be seen well. In short, five acts ended and our eyes got tired from watching enough [...].[211]

But the Moscow edition of the newspaper *Golos*[212] also gives us a very detailed article about the arrival of the Shah of Iran to Moscow, and in it is to be found very important theatrical information:

> In the evening, His Highness was at the Bolshoi Theatre, where the ballet *Magic Slipper* was performed. Before the start of the performance, His Majesty; He entered the Governor General's place accompanied by the Governor General, Adjutant General Menshikov and four high-ranking officials of the Iranian government. The music of the Iranian National marching band began to play, and the many choice spectators who had filled the hall stood up and welcomed the King of Iran. Iranian elders stood behind their server's chair throughout the performance. The great imperial grandstands, as well as the three stands to the left, were filled with the king's entourage in gold-embroidered ceremonial robes. His Highness

---

[211] Ibid, P 210.

[212] Russian Political newspaper edited and published in Saint Petersburg in 1863-1885.

Naser al Din remained in the theatre until the end of the performance [. . .].

Moscow, May 20, Tuesday.

We went to see the theatre. The actors performed very well. They performed the sinking of the ship.[213]

Moscow, May 23, Thursday.

We went to see the show with the emperor [...]. We went up the stairs and sat on the porch in front of the stage [...]. There were a lot of people there. There were many politicians, well-known people, and journalists. The theatre was on six floors. And all the floors were full of people. There were also Iranians. In the middle of the hall, there was a very beautiful and large chandelier that worked with gas. This theatre was smaller than the Moscow Theatre. Moscow singers were better [...]. They didn't act well [...].[214]

213 Naser al din shah, Edited by Majid Abd Amin, *Diary of Naser al-Din Shah Qajar the first trip in Europe*, [Rūznāmah-'i khāṭirāt-i Nāṣir al-Dīn Shāh Qājār : az Shavvāl-i 1288 tā Ẕīḥijjah-], 212.
214 Ibid 217.

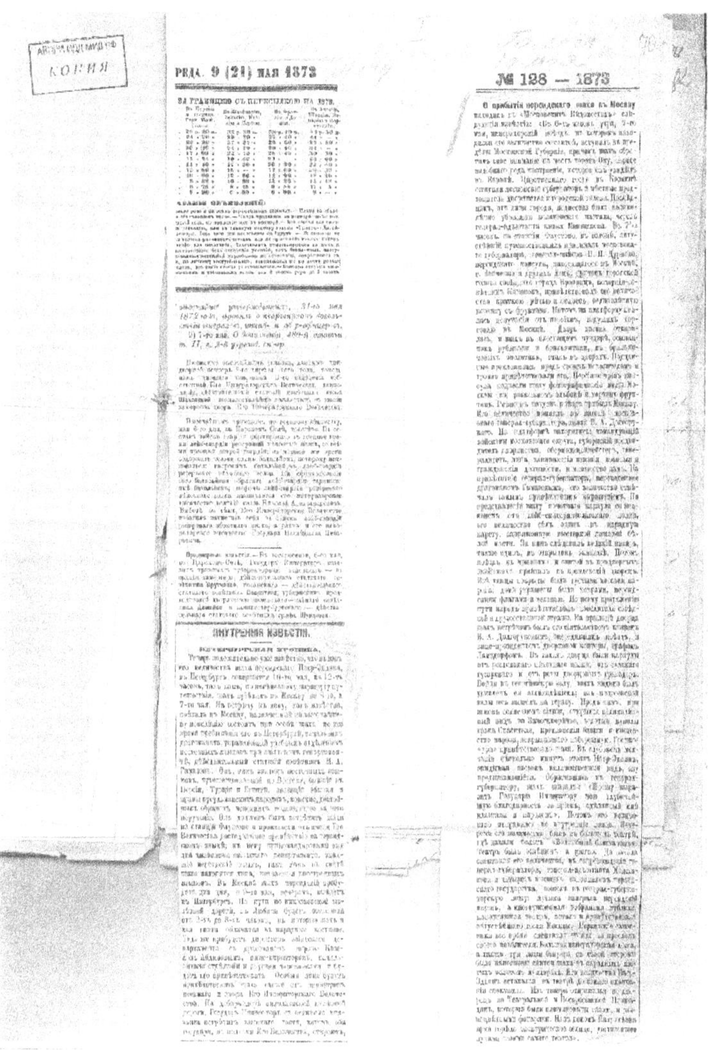

РЕДА. 9 (21) мая 1873

№ 128 — 1873

О прибытіи персидскаго шаха въ Москву

ВНУТРЕННІЯ ИЗВѢСТІЯ.

Fig. 36. The news of Naser al-Din shah's arrival in the city of Moscow, the ballet "Magic Slipper", Archive of Foreign Policy of the Russian Empire (AVPRI)

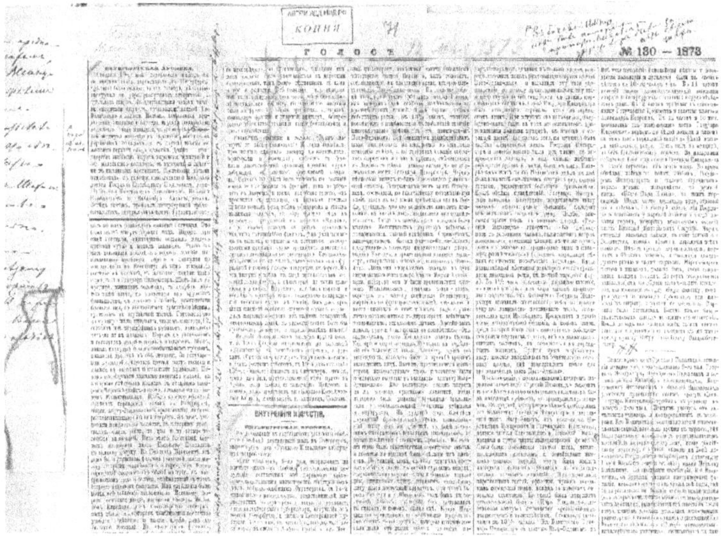
ГОЛОСЪ

№ 130 — 1873

Fig. 37. The news of Naser al-Din shah's arrival in the city of Moscow, the ballet Le Roi Candaule, Archive of Foreign Policy of the Russian Empire (AVPRI)

According to the *Golos* newspaper, Naser al-Din Shah, together with the Emperor and several Iranian and Russian political and military dignitaries, watched the ballet *Le Roi Candaule*. The interesting thing about this award ceremony was the presence of students from military colleges and military schools who came to the hall to see the Shah of Iran. Before the ballet, the orchestra played the Iranian national anthem.

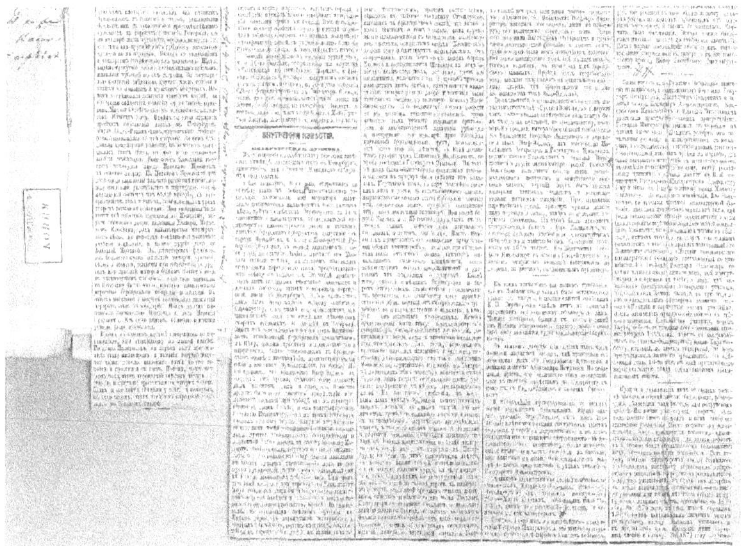

Fig. 38. The news of Naser al-Din shah's arrival in the city of Moscow, the ballet Le Roi Candaule, Archive of Foreign Policy of the Russian Empire (AVPRI)

However, the newspaper we obtained from the Berlin archives confirms the information from the Shah's travel book and the *Golos* newspaper and gives further details. The St. Petersburg *Journal* (3rd column, above) reports that the Czar, together with the Emperor of Russia and his entourage, attended the ballet *Le Roi Candaule* at eight-thirty in the Great Theatre of St. Petersburg and at ten-thirty that evening, when the ballet was over, returned to their lodgings in an open-air carriage amid the crowd.

> St. Petersburg, May 24, Saturday.
>
> After dinner we went to the Mikhailovsky Theatre. The emperor and others were not there. We sat in the last box. This theatre had six floors and was smaller than the previous one, but it was much nicer [...]. We were close

> to the stage [...]. The men were singing songs; it was like Karim Shirees Luti and France. There was a woman from Sweden who was very good on the rope [...]. The actors were doing strange things. Some of them were walking on goat balls and throwing some things into the air [...].[215]

According to the information of the newspaper *Golos* the king of Iran participated in the performance of acrobats and a magician at the Mikhailovsky Theatre with his entourage at around ten o'clock in the evening, he was very pleased with it. He especially liked acrobatics and cycling. We heard that Naser al-Din Shah received a magnificent vase as a gift from the Tsar, and upon accepting it; he said that he would keep this precious gift as a memory of his meeting with the Tsar and his stay in Russia. The Shah of Iran also gave a gift to the Tsar, which included a hookah decorated with diamonds and precious stones.

> St. Petersburg, May 25, Sunday
>
> After dinner, we went to the big theater; the emperor was also there [...]. The performance started [...]. They danced a lot in different ways [...]. I didn't like it [...]. It was a bit boring [...]."
>
> But in the newspaper [...] it is stated that: His Majesty was happy to see the big theatre where the ballet *Camargo*[216] was performed.

---

[215] Ibid 223.

[216] Ballet in three acts and nine scenes, music by Ludwig Minkus .choreography: Marius Petipa .

Fig. 39. The news of Naser al-Din shah's arrival in the city of Saint Petersburg, the ballet Le Roi Candaule, Political archive and historical service, Berlin.

> Kronstadt, May 29, Thursday.
>
> [...]. We all went to the theater [...]. We sat in the room near the stage. The emperor and the wife of the crown prince were next to us. The theater had three floors and was very beautiful [...]. On the lower floor, the nobles and elders of the country were sitting [...]. They performed *Don Quixote* [...]. It was very good [...]. The girls wore beautiful clothes. They were dancing [...]. We liked it very much.[217]

The newspaper *Golos* confirms the Shah's account of the last performance he saw before leaving for Germany, writing:

> The ballet *Don Quixote* was performed in this theatre. The hall was well lit and the entrance, staircase and foyer were decorated with the most magnificent plants and flowers. In the aisles there was a buffet for the guests. During the first intermission, the emperor, the king and the members of the imperial family drank tea in the halls next to the royal throne. The Shah's attendants served the tea at the stalls on the first floor. After the performance, the king and his companions left for St. Petersburg.

The King of Persia went to Germany after his detailed visit to Russia. Most of his observations in Germany are of royal buildings, universities, aquariums and zoos. But here too, he did not neglect to see shows and went to the Theatre.

---

[217] Naser al din shah, Edited by Majid Abd Amin, *Diary of Naser al-Din Shah Qajar the first trip in Europe*, [Rūznāmah-'i khāṭirāt-i Nāṣir al-Dīn Shāh Qājār : az Shavvāl-i 1288 tā Ẕīḥijjah], 234

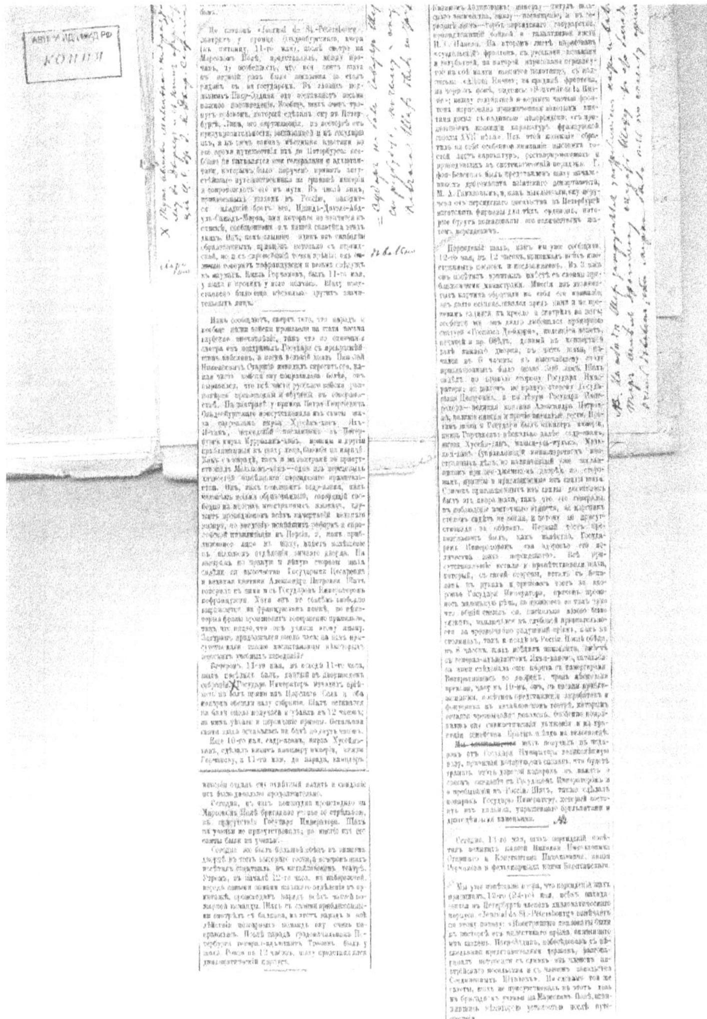

Fig. 40. The news of Naser al-Din shah's arrival in the city of Saint Petersburg, Mikhailovsky Theatre Archive of Foreign Policy of the Russian Empire (AVPRI)

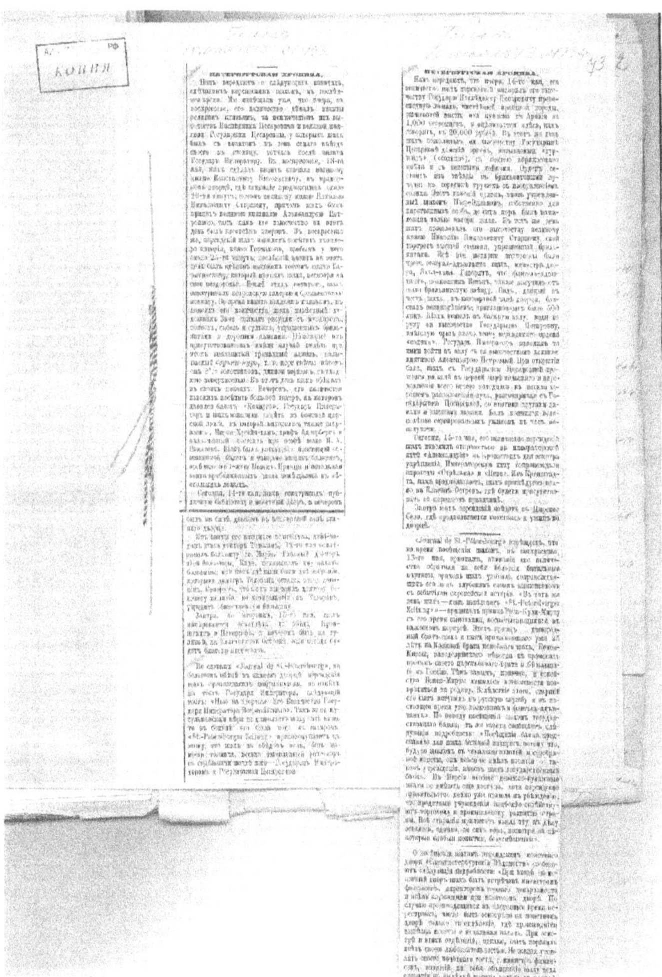

Fig. 41. The news of Naser al-Din shah's arrival in the city of Saint Petersburg, the ballet of Camargo, Archive of Foreign Policy of the Russian Empire (AVPRI)

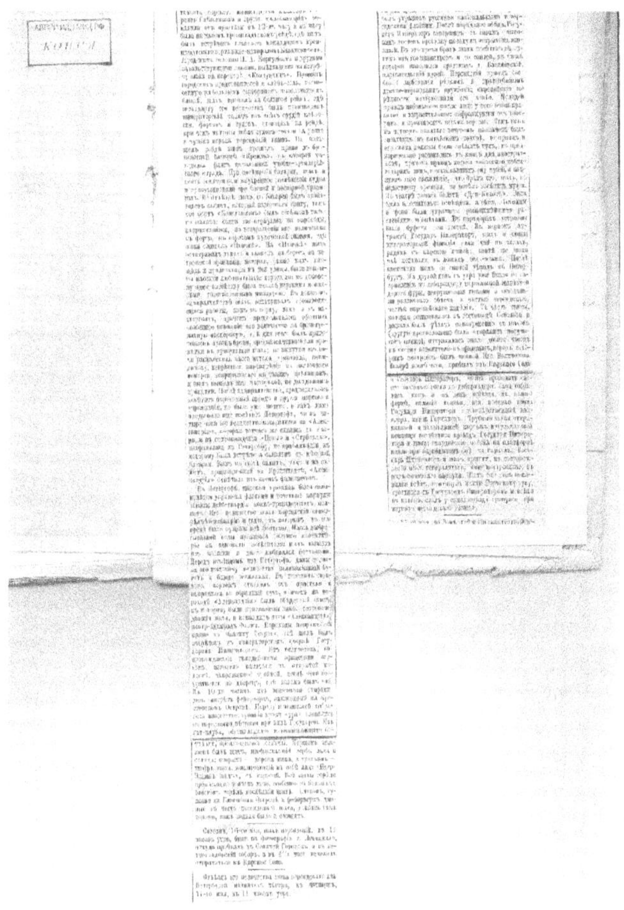

Fig. 42. The news of Naser al-Din shah's arrival in the city of Kronstadt, The ballet of Don Quixote, Archive of Foreign Policy of the Russian Empire (AVPRI)

Berlin 1873

We have two different types of information about the Shah's trip to Berlin. The first source of information is Naser al-Din Shah's diary, and the second is from the Berlin City Archives. A very interesting point is that some of the information presented in the document obtained from the Berlin archive was either not written in the Shah's diary or was omitted from it. At any rate, we narrate both these pieces of information.

Naser al-Din Shah and his companions arrived in Berlin on the first of June. It is mentioned in the Shah's diary that on the first day of their arrival in Berlin, they did not do anything special and stayed at their residence. But in the document obtained from the archives of the city of Berlin, it is mentioned that the Shah was accompanied on his journey by thirty-seven persons (members of his family, officials, and generals) and thirteen or sixteen servants. On the first evening, there was a gala performance in the royal opera house, to which the entire diplomatic corps was invited. A ballet, *Aladin*, was shown.

> June 4 Wednesday.
>
> [...] After dinner we went to the theater. This theatre has four floors but is very small. The crown prince was also the chancellor. We are in the mud [...]. It was a good performance. The last act was like the garden of Versailles and the coronation ceremony [...]. They had made the people of the show look like the people of the palace [...]. They were the same [...]. It was very good [...].[218]

The document that came to us from the archives of Berlin refers to a royal ballet on the fourth day, which was after dinner, Naser al Din Shah was accompanied by other political figures of Iran, as well as His Highness the Shah of Germany.

---

218 Naser al din shah, Edited by Majid Abd Amin, *Diary of Naser al-Din Shah Qajar the first trip in Europe*, [Rūznāmah-'i khāṭirāt-i Nāṣir al-Dīn Shāh Qājār : az Shavvāl-i 1288 tā Ẕīḥijjah-], 251

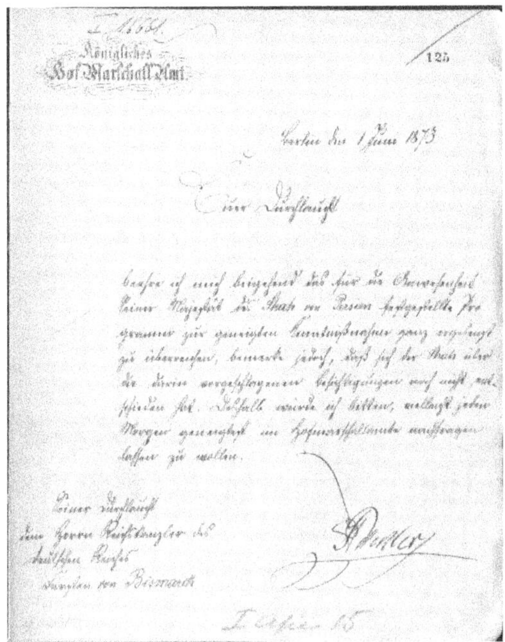

Königliches
Hof-Marschall-Amt.

125

Fig. 43. The news of Naser al-Din shah's arrival in the city of Berlin, the ballet of Aladin, Political archive and historical service, Berlin.

In the continuation of the same document, he also briefly mentioned the theatre that Naser al-Din Shah and his companions visited on the fifth day, in the city of Babolsberg, but did not go into its details.[219]

219 Not that this document says that Naser al din Shah and his companions went to see the theater in New Place after visiting the Potsdam Palace.

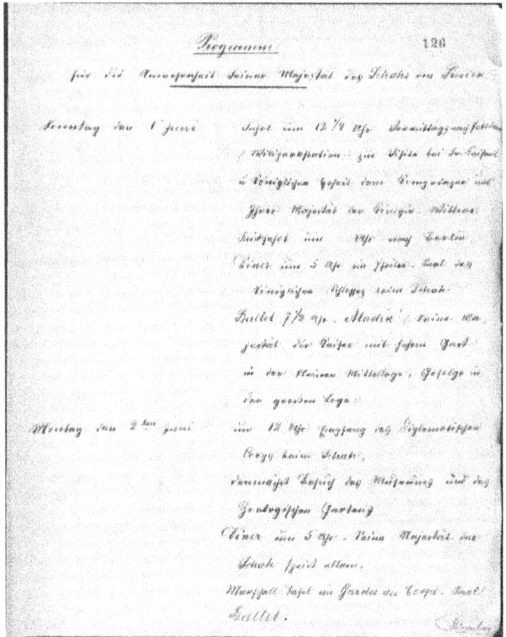

Fig. 44. The news of Naser al-Din shah's arrival in the city of Berlin, the ballet of Aladin Political archive and historical service, Berlin.

In the continuation of his journey, the Shah of Iran now entered Belgium, and after passing through various cities, entered the city of Spa.

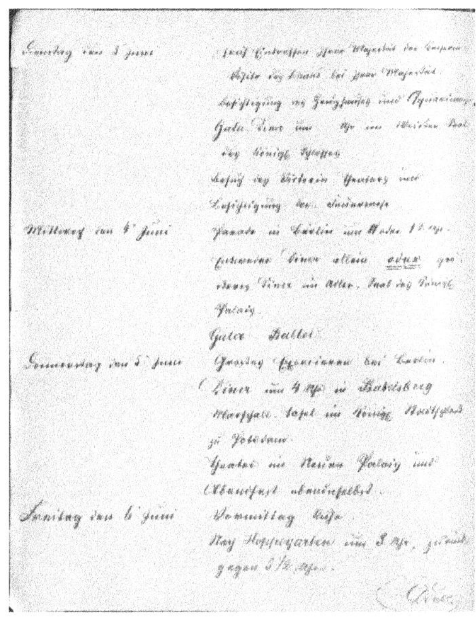

Fig. 45. The news of Naser al-Din shah's arrival in the city of Berlin, Political archive and historical service, Berlin.

Fig.46 The news of Naser al-Din shah's arrival in the city of Berlin, 44. Political archive and historical service, Berlin.

Belgium, Spa June 1873.

The newspaper *Courrier de L' Escaut* (number 164) dated June 13, 1873, has an article titled "Le voyage du Shah" about the Shah's trip, wherein is discussed how the Shah of Iran came to European countries. This article, which is intriguing in its own right, discusses the characteristics and behaviors of the Shah and Iranians, as well as the economic challenges in Iran that prompted the Shah to embark on his journey. And it indicates that the king is likely considering a significant change for Iranian society and... But the Shah writes in his diary:

> June 16 Monday.
>
> We had a most distasteful and unhygienic dinner [...]. We went to the theater. It was very small. It was even smaller than the Astrakhan theatre, but it was very beautiful [...]. A man and a woman talked in French [...]. It was a love game [...]. We didn't like it [...].
>
> [....]We went for three or four hours until I reached Brussels [...]. Brussels is the capital of Belgium [...]. This country is very free and independent [...]. The king has no authority [...]. Everything is under the jurisdiction of the parliament [...]. The journalists are also very free [...].[220]

---

220 Naser al din shah, Edited by Majid Abd Amin, *Diary of Naser al-Din Shah Qajar the first trip in Europe*, [Rūznāmah-'i khāṭirāt-i Nāṣir al-Dīn Shāh Qājār : az Shavvāl-i 1288 tā Ẕīḥijjah-i], 280

Document No. 47

Title of the Document:

Courrier de L'Escaut Report on Naser al-Din Shah's European Journey and His Arrival in Spa

Date:

13 June 1873

Repository:

Belgian Newspaper Archives

Type of Document:

Press Report and Political Commentary

Description of the Document:

This document consists of an article entitled *Le voyage du Shah* ("The Shah's Journey"), published in issue no. 164 of the Belgian newspaper *Courrier de L'Escaut* during Naser al-Din Shah's first European tour. Written shortly after the Shah's arrival in the Belgian city of Spa, the article provides both a report of the royal visit and a broader commentary on the political, social, and economic conditions of Qajar Persia.

In addition to describing the Shah's presence in Europe, the author discusses aspects of his character and leadership while examining the economic difficulties and administrative challenges facing Iran during the period. The article suggests that the monarch's journey was motivated not only by diplomatic considerations but also by a desire to observe European institutions and achievements firsthand. The author further speculates that the experience acquired during the tour could contribute to significant social and administrative changes within Iran.

The importance of this document lies in its reflection of contemporary European perceptions of Persia and its ruler during the nineteenth century. It demonstrates how sections of the European press viewed Iran as a country confronting substantial internal challenges while simultaneously seeking greater engagement with the modern political and cultural developments of Europe. As such, the article provides valuable insight into Western interpretations of Naser al-Din Shah's travels and the broader process of modernization associated with the Qajar period.

Source:

Courrier de L'Escaut, No. 164, "Le voyage du Shah," 13 June 1873.

Fig. 47. The news of Naser al-Din shah's arrival in the city of Spa in the newspaper Courrier de L'Escaut, 1873.

> Brussels 1873,
>
> June 17, Tuesday.
>
> Tonight we went to a traditional theater [...]. We went up and sat in the lodge [...]. Myself, the king, and the chancellor [...]. We sat next to each other. All Iranian and foreign princes were in official attire. The theatre was six stories high and very beautiful. It was no less than the great theatre of Peter [...]. This theatre belongs to the opera house. That is, they sang songs and played good music. Ugly men sang very badly. Sometimes women also answered. It was like Iranian songs. We liked it. Then they danced a lot [...]. It was ballet. They were dancing well, but it took a long time [...]. We got tired [...] It's finally over.[221]

Naser al Din Shah continued his journey, this time on June 19; he entered England by route of sea and received a unique welcome. During his relatively long stay in England, he visited many cultural and artistic places. Among these places were the Royal Albert and other theatres.

London, England, 1873

The Shah states in his diary:

> June 22, Sunday.
>
> At night we wore traditional clothes and the carriage [. . .]. We went to the theater [which] was a six-story theatre with many boxes [...]. There were many people.

---

[221] Ibid 285.

> The theatre is very leafy. It has six floors. They show me very good scenes. A garden and tree and [...]. There was a singer who came from Paris, she sang very well, she was a beautiful woman and they had paid a lot of money to invite her. Another one from Canada sang very well [. . .]. The theatre took us a long time to get tired. I was going crazy [...].[222]
>
> July 4, Friday.
>
> We went to the Drury Lane theatre at night. It was very far away. There were many people in the street. The Crown Prince of England was waiting for us there. He greeted us very warmly. We went and sat down. Prince Alfred also came. Opera and ballet were both there. They sang and danced well. The dancers were very well dressed. The theatre has five floors and is very nice, although it is a little small. A famous singer named Nelson came from Sweden, he sings well. The crown prince brought him and we talked a little [...].[223]

But during his relatively long stay in England, the Shah of Iran was more involved in political and official meetings, and he took the time to go to the concert theatre. He visited numerous luxurious buildings, museums, and palaces before heading to France.

---

[222] Ibid 301.
[223] Ibid 339.

Paris, France, 1873[224]

July 19.

Naser al-Din shah, who until then had read and heard a lot about Paris, finds himself in Paris this time and is overwhelmed by the beauty there. During his stay in Paris, he visits all the sights of the city, including museums and palaces. In one part of the travelogue, he looks at the Mermaid opera:

> Paris has many theatres. One evening we went to the big theatre where all the ambassadors and ministers were there with their wives. Iranian princes were also there. The theatre was very big and had five floors. With very big and spectacular lights. There were very many people who came. The dancers and singers danced and sang very well, especially when they showed the underwater world. The mermaids danced very well.[225]

Torino, Italy.

25 July 1873.

---

224 Regarding Naser al din Shah's trip to France, the information is from his diary. But in his travel letter, unfortunately, he did not write the dates of the days he was there and the information was written in one place. Therefore, the dates mentioned in this book are possible and based on my own guess.

225 Naser al din shah, Edited by Majid Abd Amin, *Diary of Naser al-Din Shah Qajar the first trip in Europe*, [Rūznāmah-'i khāṭirāt-i Nāṣir al-Dīn Shāh Qājār : az Shavvāl-i 1288 tā Ẕīḥijjah-], 373

The Iranian king and his companions continue their travels and after passing through Switzerland, they enter Italian territory and the city of Turin. In his travelogue, the Shah talks about the beauty of the road and the city of Turin, and how just two nights later, he went to see the opera *Norma* by Bellini[226] at the *Teatro Regio* di Torino. He says in his diary:[227]

[...]

On the other hand, the story in the newspaper *La stampa,*[228], published on July 25, 1873, again devotes a column to the visit of the Shah of Iran to Turin:

> Arrival of the Shah of Persia
>
> It must be said that the preparations for the grand reception of the Shah were truly splendid and executed flawlessly. From the Royal Palace, where a company of the National Guard had gathered, a procession extended to Piazza S. Carlo, consisting of infantry units. In Piazza S. Carlo, the artillery with its canons was stationed, while in Via Rama and Piazza Carlo Felice, infantry and Bersaglieri troops were lined up. At the departure station, the King's Cuirassiers were in their splendid uniforms, and the *Carabinieri*[229] ensured that all access points to the railway were clear. Within the station, representatives of all branches of the military, the Prefect and the Provincial Deputation, the

---

226 (1801-1835) Vincenzo Salvatore Carmelo Francesco Bellini was an Italian opera composer.

227 Naser al din shah, Edited by Majid Abd Amin, *Diary of Naser al-Din Shah Qajar the first trip in Europe*, [Rūznāmah-'i khāṭirāt-i Nāṣir al-Dīn Shāh Qājār : az Shavvāl-i 1288 tā Z̲īḥijjah], 396

228 La Stampa Is an Italian daily newspaper published in Turin, 1 February 1867.

229 Italian Police

Mayor and the City Council, all the Senators and Deputies present in Turin, as well as high-ranking Court officials, and many other invited guests had been in their positions since eight o'clock in the morning. A proclamation by the mayor announced the arrival of the Shah at eight. At fifteen past eight, Prince Umberto was announced. The

Document No. 48

Title of the Document:

Report on the Arrival of Naser al-Din Shah in Turin during His First European Journey

Date: 25 July 1873

Repository: Archivio Storico La Stampa, Turin, Italy

Type of Document: Newspaper Report

Description of the Document:

This document consists of a detailed report published in the Italian newspaper *La Stampa* on the occasion of Naser al-Din Shah's arrival in Turin during his first European journey in 1873. The article provides a comprehensive account of the elaborate preparations undertaken by the Italian authorities to receive the Persian monarch, describing the participation of members of the royal family, government ministers, military units, municipal officials, and representatives of the Italian parliament.

Particular attention is devoted to the ceremonial reception organized at the railway station, where King Vittorio Emanuele II personally welcomed the Shah upon his arrival. The report records the presence of Prince Umberto, the Duke of Aosta, senior ministers, and numerous dignitaries, while also describing the military honors, public celebrations, and the enthusiastic response of the population. The article further notes the procession that escorted the Shah through the city and the extensive illuminations and festivities organized in his honor.

Of particular interest is the newspaper's announcement of the gala performance scheduled for the same evening at the Teatro Regio di Torino, where Bellini's opera *Norma* was to be performed before the royal guests and members of the court. The report therefore offers valuable evidence of the close connection between diplomatic ceremony and cultural spectacle during the Shah's European tour.

The importance of this document lies in its portrayal of the extraordinary reception accorded to Naser al-Din Shah by the Italian monarchy and state authorities. It illustrates the diplomatic significance attributed to the Persian ruler's visit and provides insight into the ways in which the European press presented the Shah's journey to contemporary audiences. The article also sheds light on the role of opera and public ceremonial culture in nineteenth-century Italy as instruments of royal representation and international diplomacy.

Source:

La Stampa, "Arrivee dello Scià di Persia," 25 July 1873. Archivio Storico La Stampa, Turin, Italy.

Fig. 48. Visit of Norma Oprah by Naser al-Din shah, Journal of LA STAMPA, Archive of Turin, Italy, 1873.

Prime Minister, the Ministers of Foreign Affairs, Agriculture, and Commerce went to greet him. At eight twenty-five, the King, the Duke of Aosta, and the Prince of Carignano entered the station and received the homage of the authorities. At twelve past eight, the electric bell signaled the arrival of the royal train in Collegno. King Vittorio Emanuele, followed by the Royal Princes, left the waiting room and walked under the grand arch. At eight forty-two, the royal convoy, led by Commander Bachelet, the head of traffic, and an inspector, entered the station. The first carriage contained the Deputation that had gone to Bardonecchia to welcome the Shah on behalf of the King. The second carriage held the Shah's personal entourage. In the third carriage, stood the Shah, currently the guest of the King of Italy and the city of Turin. He wore the Persian headdress adorned with a renowned diamond-encrusted plume, along with a tunic embellished with enormous diamonds on his chest. As the train came to a stop, Vittorio Emanuele removed his kepi and stood in front of the royal carriage. The Shah saw him and uncovered his head. Meanwhile, an employee opened the door, and the Shah hurriedly approached the King, who also took a step forward to embrace and kiss him twice. After welcoming him in French, the King introduced Prince Umberto, the Duke of Aosta, and the Prince of Carignano. They followed with warm handshakes. In the first of the Court carriages (masterpieces of artistic taste), the Shah, the King of Italy, Prince Umberto, and a high-ranking Persian dignitary took their seats. In the second carriage, the Grand Vizier, the Duke of Aosta, and other Persian dignitaries were seated. In the third carriage, the Prince of Carignano sat with other foreign guests. In the fourth carriage, the Minister of Agriculture and Commerce and two Persian dignitaries were seated. In the fifth carriage, Minghetti, Visconti-Venosta, and another Persian dignitary took their places. In the sixth carriage, stood the aides-de-camp of the Shah and the King of Italy. In the seventh carriage were seated the dignitaries of the Royal Household. Numerous other carriages carried the Shah's entourage, authorities, and the City Council, among others. The streets and squares traversed by the procession were splendidly illuminated. The fireworks in Piazza Carlo Felice and the electric light in Piazza Castello created a breathtaking effect that dazzled the onlookers. All the military bands played the Persian anthem, and the immense, indescribable crowd erupted in applause without pause. Today, official presentations and receptions will take place, followed by a grand banquet at the Court, to which all the authorities have been invited. In the evening, there will be a gala performance at the Royal Theater with the participation of the entire Court. They will perform *Norma* with the tenor Urban and, organized by the company, two special ballets in which the entire ballet corps of the Royal School will take part. It is anticipated to be a brilliant

> evening. The *Gazzetta del Popolo* is pleased to announce that the health of the Duchess of Aosta is improving. And we are delighted to reiterate this announcement.

Austria 1873

In continuation of his adventures in Europe, the Shah of Iran reached Austria, which was one of the most important centres of music and opera in Europe. He did not miss any opportunity to see the theatre, opera and concerts:

> Vienna, August 5, Tuesday
>
> At half past nine we have to go to the Empire theatre. In the street when people saw us they got excited and greeted us. This theatre is very special; for its interior design they used a lot of gold and marble. The lights work with electricity. The building is of five floors. In this theatre they put on popular shows.[230]

[230] Naser al din shah, Edited by Majid Abd Amin, *Diary of Naser al-Din Shah Qajar the first trip in Europe*, [Rūznāmah-'i khāṭirāt-i Nāṣir al-Dīn Shāh Qājār : az Shavvāl-i 1288 tā Ẕīḥijjah-], 424

Document No. 49

Title of the Document:

Newspaper Report on Naser al-Din Shah's Visit to Vienna

Date: 9 June 1874

Repository: Austrian Newspaper Archive, Vienna, Austria

Type of Document: Newspaper Report

Description of the Document:

This document consists of a report published in the Viennese newspaper *Wiener Abendpost* concerning Naser al-Din Shah's visit to the Austrian capital. The article reflects the considerable public and press interest generated by the Persian monarch's presence in Vienna, one of the most important political, cultural, and artistic centres of nineteenth-century Europe.

The report presents the Shah's visit within the broader context of the official receptions and public ceremonies organized in his honour. As in many contemporary European newspaper accounts, the article emphasizes both the diplomatic significance of the visit and the curiosity that the Persian ruler inspired among the Austrian public. Such reports played an important role in shaping European perceptions of Persia and its monarchy, presenting the Shah as both a political figure and a distinguished foreign guest.

The importance of this document lies in its illustration of the attention devoted by the Austrian press to Naser al-Din Shah's European travels and his encounters with Vienna's cultural institutions. Read alongside the Shah's own travel diary, the article provides valuable evidence of the interaction between the Persian monarch and the cultural life of Vienna, a city renowned for its theatres, opera houses, and musical traditions. As a contemporary source, it offers insight into the public reception of the Shah and the role of the press in documenting and interpreting his travels across Europe.

Particularly noteworthy is the fact that the article was published approximately one year after Naser al-Din Shah's first visit to Vienna in 1873. This suggests that the memory of the Shah's presence in the Austrian capital continued to attract public and journalistic attention long after the event itself. The publication of such retrospective accounts indicates that the Persian monarch's visit was not regarded merely as a passing diplomatic occasion, but rather as a noteworthy episode in the cultural and political relations between Persia and Europe. Consequently, the document provides evidence of the lasting impact that the Shah's European journeys had on the Austrian press and on contemporary European perceptions of Qajar Iran.

Source:

Wiener Abendpost, Vienna, 9 June 1874, Austrian Newspaper Archive, Vienna, Austria.

Fig. 49. A retelling of the Naser al-Din Shah's arrival in Vienna, Journal of Wiener Abendpost, Archive of Vienna, Austria, 1874.

From Naser al din Shah's information it is clear how much he paid attention to the architecture of the buildings and to the actors, perhaps because the type of show was unknown to him. However, he explained well in his travel memoir all kinds of entertainments that he attended, and he found them very interesting.

Well until after a year, the Vienna newspapers were writing about Naser al Din Shah's travels in Europe: most of the information was obtained from the travel memoirs that he personally had written. Many of these performances were staged at Schönbrunn Palace in Vienna.

Naser was very impressed by a ballet that he says he attended four times, fascinated by the spectacular forms, which were completely new to him, and by the buildings, which he found magnificent. Hence his interest in the characteristic architecture of the Vienna Opera, which he considered the most beautiful compared to the others he had seen in Europe, with its five ranks of boxes, a very beautiful curtain, and a royal box where the German and Austrian princes used to sit. He judged that the opera had very pleasant music, enriched by the different colors of the scene and the clothes of the fantastic and mythological characters.

Document No. 50

Title of the Document:

Official List of Naser al-Din Shah's Entourage during His Stay in Vienna

Date:

July–August 1873

Repository:

Austrian State Archives, Vienna, Austria

Type of Document:

Official Administrative and Ceremonial Record

Description of the Document:

This document contains part of the official list of individuals accompanying Naser al-Din Shah during his stay in Vienna in July and August 1873, as part of his first European journey. Prepared by the Austrian authorities, the record identifies the members of the Persian royal delegation and specifies their official positions and ranks within the Qajar court.

The section presented here is devoted to princes, ministers, and senior officials of the Persian government. Among those listed are several prominent members of the Qajar royal family and high-ranking statesmen, including Heshmat al-Dowleh, Ezz al-Dowleh, Amin al-Sultan, Nosrat al-Dowleh, and Amin al-Dowleh. The document demonstrates the scale and diplomatic importance of the Shah's European mission, which required the participation of a large entourage composed of royal relatives, ministers, military officers, secretaries, interpreters, and court officials.

The importance of this document lies in its detailed record of the composition of the Persian delegation during one of the most significant diplomatic journeys of the Qajar period. Examined alongside the Shah's travel memoirs, it provides valuable insight into the administrative organization of the royal tour and the individuals who accompanied the monarch during his encounters with European political and cultural institutions. The document also reflects the careful attention paid by Austrian authorities to the reception and management of the Persian court during its stay in Vienna.

Source:

Austrian State Archives, Vienna. *Gefolge Seiner Majestät des Schah von Persien während der allerhöchsten Anwesenheit in Wien im Monate Juli und August 1873.*

Fig. 50. List of companions of Naser al-Din Shah in Vienna 1, Archive of Vienna, Austria, August 1873.

Document No. 51

Title of the Document:

Official List of Naser al-Din Shah's Entourage and Program Arrangements during His Stay in Vienna

Date: August 1873

Repository: Austrian State Archives, Vienna, Austria

Type of Document: Official Administrative and Ceremonial Record

Description of the Document:

This document forms part of the official records prepared by the Austrian authorities during Naser al-Din Shah's stay in Vienna in August 1873. In addition to listing members of the Persian royal entourage, including court officials, military officers, servants, interpreters, and administrative personnel, the document provides valuable information concerning the organization of the Shah's visit and the arrangements made for his reception in the Austrian capital.

The record illustrates the scale of the Persian delegation and reflects the diplomatic importance attached to the Shah's presence in Vienna. The large number of accompanying officials demonstrates the complexity of the royal tour and the careful planning required for the movement and accommodation of the Qajar court during its European journey.

Particularly significant is the evidence the document provides regarding the cultural program organized during the Shah's stay. Contemporary records indicate that the schedule prepared for the Persian monarch was divided into two distinct sections. The first consisted of official ceremonies, receptions, and events arranged by the Austrian court and government. The second included activities specifically requested by Naser al-Din Shah himself, many of which involved visits to theatres, opera houses, concerts, and other artistic performances.

Examined alongside the Shah's travel memoirs, the document reveals the extent of his interest in European performing arts and architecture. Throughout his travels, he repeatedly attended theatrical performances and musical productions, often commenting on the design of theatre buildings, stage machinery, costumes, and scenic effects. Vienna, as one of Europe's foremost cultural capitals, offered the Shah an opportunity to experience artistic forms that were largely unfamiliar to him, leaving a lasting impression that is reflected throughout his travel writings.

Source:

Austrian State Archives, Vienna. Official List of Naser al-Din Shah's Entourage and Program Arrangements during His Stay in Vienna, August 1873.

Fig. 51. List of companions of Naser al-Din Shah in Vienna 2, Archive of Vienna, Austria, August 1873.

From his travel reports, it is clear that Naser al Din Shah was influenced by the European theatre and the architecture of its theatre buildings.

In every trip that the Shah made to different European countries, a program was usually arranged by the host to welcome the Iranian monarch, and at the top of these programs were performances and concerts. But a very important and interesting point in the Shah's trip to Austria was his request to see some performances.

A look at Document 50 shows that the program prepared for the Shah of Iran was divided into two parts. The upper part contains a list of ceremonies planned by the host for the king, while the lower portion contains a list of programs planned at the request of the king himself.

Document No. 52

Title of the Document:

Official Schedule of Naser al-Din Shah's Stay and Activities in Vienna

Date: July–August 1873

Repository: Austrian State Archives, Vienna, Austria

Type of Document: Official Administrative and Ceremonial Program

Description of the Document:

This document contains the official schedule prepared for Naser al-Din Shah's stay in Vienna during his first European journey in 1873. Compiled by the Austrian authorities, it records the official meetings, ceremonial receptions, and cultural activities organized for the Persian monarch and his entourage during their residence in the Austrian capital. The document is divided into two distinct sections. The upper portion contains the ceremonies, audiences, and official engagements arranged by the Austrian court and government, while the lower section lists activities and events specifically requested by the Shah himself.

The importance of this document lies in the insight it provides into Naser al-Din Shah's personal interest in European performing arts. The schedule demonstrates that his attendance at theatres, operas, concerts, and other artistic performances was not merely the result of official hospitality offered by his hosts. Rather, it reveals that the Shah actively sought opportunities to experience European cultural life and personally requested access to a number of artistic events during his stay in Vienna. This suggests that his familiarity with Western theatrical and musical traditions predated his arrival in Austria and that he consciously pursued these experiences throughout his travels.

From the perspective of Persian theatre history, the document is particularly significant because it also sheds light on the individuals who accompanied the Shah to many of these performances. Several members of the royal entourage later played important roles in the cultural and intellectual life of Qajar Iran. Figures such as Mohammad Hasan Khan Sanie al-Dowleh (Etemad al-Saltaneh), Mehdi Gholi Khan, and Naser al-Molk were among those who witnessed European theatrical and musical productions firsthand. Their exposure to modern theatre buildings, stage technology, dramatic literature, and performance practices contributed to the transmission of European theatrical ideas into Iran during the late nineteenth century.

Examined alongside the Shah's travel memoirs, this document provides valuable evidence of the cultural dimension of the Qajar monarch's European journeys. It demonstrates that these visits were not limited to diplomatic encounters and official ceremonies, but also functioned as important opportunities for artistic observation and cultural exchange. Consequently, the document offers a unique perspective on the role of European travel in shaping the intellectual and theatrical transformations that emerged in Iran during the later Qajar period.

Source:

Austrian State Archives, Vienna. Official Schedule of Naser al-Din Shah's Stay and Activities in Vienna, 1873.

Fig. 52.The schedule of Naser al-Din Shah's visit to Vienna, Archive of Vienna, Austria, 1873.

This point shows that the Shah's familiarity with Western shows did not depend on his travels. He already knew these shows and made an effort to watch them during his trips to the West. In any case, after his three trips to Europe, the Shah, along with his companions, whether knowingly or unknowingly, became the vehicles of significant changes in the history of Iran during the Qajar period.

Another important point in the documents of Naser al-Din Shah's trip to Vienna is the mention of the names of all his companions in theaters, operas and concerts. Among these people are those who were involved in the performing arts. And both before and after the Shah's travels, they created and produced plays. Certainly, with the knowledge they had received from the European theater and considering all their previous knowledge about Iranian theater, these people were able to have a great influence on the new theater imported to Iran. As can be seen from the above document, the names of the political figures from the time of Naser al-Din Shah can be seen who accompanied the Shah in every performance and concert. A clear example of this is the person of Mohammad Hasan Khan Sanie al-Dowleh (Etemad al-Saltaneh), whose influence on the theater of the Qajar era is obvious to everyone. Apart from Etemad al-Saltaneh, Mehdi Goli Khan, who was a passionate classical musician and was well, acquainted with Persian theater and probably paid much attention to the European shows that he participated in with the Shah because he knew some European languages. Also, Naser al-Molk, who studied at Oxford, knew some European languages and translated some of Shakespeare's texts[231].

---

[231] The Shah of Iran made his European trips to several other countries and returned to Iran. As we said that he traveled to Europe two more times and continued his adventures in 1878 and 1889 and appeared again in other trips. Our intention here was to mention examples of his initial meeting with the western show, which led to changes in the Iranian show.

1. The travels of Mozafar al-din Shah

But the adventures of the Qajarians did not end there. After Mozafar al-Din Shah ascended to the royal throne, he continued in his father's footsteps by embarking on exploration trips. So the visit to the external and enchanting manifestations of Western culture and civilization continued. Mozafar al-Din Shah not only inherited the royal throne and a penchant for fun and entertainment, but also his father's love for Farang (European) travel. Therefore, during his ten-year reign, he frequently traveled to Europe, claiming to seek treatment for his rheumatism by using the mineral and healing waters of the Alps. in an era when the country's treasury was emptier than during any other, and the current affairs of the country were being managed by borrowing from Russian and British banks in exchange for the granting of numerous privileges.

In any case, and although the exorbitant costs of such trips were made by borrowing from foreign powers and the lending of the country's financial resources (thus directly putting pressure on the treasury and pockets of the people), the European journies themselves were not so insignificant. Apparently on the advice of the informed English doctors treating the Shah, Mozafar al-Din Shah's initial journey took place on 12 April 1900 to the countries of Russia, Austria, Switzerland, Germany, Belgium and France and to the Alpine spa springs.

This trip, the cost of which according to Nazim al-Islam,[232] was graciously spent on entertainment, did not have any results other than creating dissatisfaction and anger among the people in the absence of the king. One of the historic events of this trip was the assassination attempt on the life of Mozafar al-Din Shah in the city of Paris. Fortunately, there

[232] Nazim-al-Islam Kermani, History *of Iranian Awakening*, [Tārīkh-i bīdārī-i Īrāniyān] Volume 1, Saeedi Sirjani's effort, (Farhang Foundation, Tehran 1967) 130.

are two books on the account of this journey: one is the travel book of Mobarake Shahanshahi, supposedly written by Mozafar al-Din Shah but actually by one of the court officials and printed in Bombay in 1903, and the other is the travel book of Zahir ad-Dawlah, written by Mirza Ali Khan Zahir ad-Dawlah, the son-in-law of Naser al-Din Shah. One of the associates of Mozafar al-Din Shah during this trip, he recorded the events of the trip from Thursday, April 12, 1900, to Sunday, November 25, 1900. During Mozafar al-Din Shah's second trip to Europe, which took place in April 1901, Russia and European countries including Austria, Prussia, Belgium, France, Italy and finally the intended destination of England were visited by the Shah and his delegation. In this trip, which was made under the pretext of treating the Shah's rheumatism, the sick but happy Shah had nothing else to do except photographing different places and landscapes, going to court dances, concerts, operas, and other shows. He spent the days listening to the speeches that were read in honor of his presence in official ceremonies and spent the nights expressing his observations and memories to his secretary Fakhr al-Molk. His memoirs that were published in the form of a book both during the Shah's lifetime and in 1942 had, in addition to receiving Gardner's garter badge by the Shah himself, a wide-ranging impact. Apparently, items like an ice cream maker, an electric cooking pot, a camera, a telephone, a gold watch, a double carriage and a hunting rifle were also souvenirs of this trip. Of proper course, and possibly based on some claims and evidence, it can be accepted that the idea of constitutionalism was also one of the other souvenirs of this trip.

As Mozaffar al-din Shah said in a decree dated the 27th of September 1906, he had the intention of establishing constitutionalism from the time of his first and second trips to Europe. The third trip of Shah Qajar took place in June 1905, accompanied by a group of fifty court servants and courtiers, to Austria, France, Belgium and Russia. A trip that took place after receiving a loan of 290,000 lira from the Royal Bank of England and without any important political achievements in a hundred days. Only a few telephones, a cinematograph camera, a sound recording and broadcasting device, and a device for displaying still images were the souvenirs of this trip. This was also prepared for the court. Although Alam al-Dawla Thaghafi did not write the report of this third trip, apparently due to the occurrence of the Constitutional Revolution and the fear of intensifying popular protests, the court refused to publish it.

Another very interesting and important point of these trips was the company of some Qajar politicians who were also very interested in seeing and learning about Western theatre. Amin al-Soltan, Hakim al-Molk, Zahir al-Molk, Mothaq al-Dawleh, Mofkham al-Dawleh, Moshir al-Molk, and several other ministers, as well as Sani al-Saltaneh, a photographer, Naser Homayun, Nadim al-Soltan, a translator, and a number of others can be mentioned among those accompanying the king on these trips.

But during the first trip of the king to Europe, in which he went to Vienna and Budapest also, some important dramatic events happened, which bear mention.

The Viennese, who were the hosts of the Shah of Iran, had prepared a partial show or a program of song and dance combined with music and drama to pay their respects to the shah and his entourage. As understanding the German language was not possible for all of them, making this program pleasant appeared difficult. But more importantly, there is no report of this side ceremony in Mozafar al-Din Shah's travelogue, and it can only be learned about by referring to Austrian government documents.

Looking at the Paré theatre program, we can understand that the element of movement in the Paré theatre shows can be seen in most of these programs. Especially according to

Document 3, it can be understood that Balt is included in the majority of Paré theatre performances.

Document No. 53

Title of the Document:

Program of the Théâtre Paré at the Imperial Court Opera Theatre, Vienna

Date:

21 September 1900

Repository:

Austrian State Archives, Vienna, Austria

Type of Document:

Official Theatre Program

Description of the Document:

This document is the cover page of the official program for the *Théâtre Paré*, a series of special court performances presented at the Imperial Court Opera Theatre in Vienna. Unlike Vienna's permanent theatrical institutions, the *Théâtre Paré* was not a regular theatre company or a permanent performance venue. Rather, it was a ceremonial theatrical enterprise organized within the framework of court festivities and intended primarily for distinguished royal and diplomatic guests visiting the Habsburg court.

The significance of this document lies in its connection to the visits of the Qajar monarchs to Austria. Available evidence suggests that performances associated with the *Théâtre Paré* were first organized in connection with Naser al-Din Shah's visit to Vienna in 1873, when Austrian authorities sought to honor the Persian monarch and his entourage through specially arranged cultural events. The tradition continued in subsequent years and was revived during the European journeys of Mozaffar al-Din Shah, becoming part of the ceremonial program prepared for the Persian court during its visits to Vienna.

As such, the *Théâtre Paré* represents an example of the Habsburg monarchy's use of theatrical culture as an instrument of diplomacy and royal representation. Through specially commissioned performances, music, dance, and visual spectacle, the Austrian court sought to display the artistic sophistication and cultural prestige of the Empire to its foreign guests. Following the final visit of Mozaffar al-Din Shah to Vienna and the changing political and cultural circumstances of the early twentieth century, the *Théâtre Paré* gradually disappeared and ceased to function as part of the court's ceremonial traditions.

Source:

Austrian State Archives, Vienna. *Théâtre Paré im K. K. Hof-Operntheater*, 21 September 1900.

Fig. 53. Program of Pare Theatre 1, Archive of Vienna, Austria, 1900.

Document No. 54

Title of the Document:

Program of Performances Presented at the Théâtre Paré during Mozaffar al-Din Shah's Visit to Vienna

Date: 21 September 1900

Repository: Austrian State Archives, Vienna, Austria

Type of Document:

Theatrical Performance Program

Description of the Document:

This document contains the program of performances presented at the *Théâtre Paré* during Mozaffar al-Din Shah's stay in Vienna in 1900. The program lists the theatrical and musical works selected for presentation before the Persian monarch and his entourage as part of the official cultural festivities organized by the Austrian court.

Among the featured productions were *Sonne und Erde* ("Sun and Earth"), a ballet in three acts, and *Vergissmeinnicht* ("Forget-Me-Not"), a theatrical work combining music, dance, and dramatic performance. The program also records the names of performers, composers, choreographers, and members of the orchestra, illustrating the scale and artistic complexity of the event.

The significance of this document lies in its demonstration of the type of theatrical entertainment considered suitable for presentation to distinguished foreign guests at the Habsburg court. The predominance of ballet, music, movement, and visual spectacle suggests a deliberate effort to overcome linguistic barriers and communicate through performance forms that could be appreciated regardless of the audience's native language. This was particularly relevant for the Persian delegation, many of whose members had limited familiarity with German.

Viewed in conjunction with contemporary travel accounts, the document provides valuable insight into the artistic environment encountered by Mozaffar al-Din Shah and the members of his entourage during their stay in Vienna. It also offers evidence of the role that theatrical performances played within the broader framework of cultural diplomacy and court ceremonial at the turn of the twentieth century.

Source:

Austrian State Archives, Vienna. Program of the *Théâtre Paré*, Imperial Court Opera Theatre, 21 September 1900.

Fig. 54. Program of Pare Theatre 2, Archive of Vienna, Austria, 1900.

Happy travels of Mozafar al-Din Shah in Austria[233]

Although travel plans to countries such as Russia, Germany and England were mainly accompanied by political meetings and diplomatic talks and dry and soulless ceremonies such as seeing army parades and visiting factories, travel plans in countries such as Austria and France boasted more sophistication and charms and created fun times for the Iranian entourage in theatres and music halls. Mozafar al-Din Shah, like his father, had an especially great interest in music and the performing arts, and he enjoyed the popular ceremony of welcoming foreign guests and rulers with happy and fun musical programs. Although he once admitted that he was more interested in ballet than opera.

In any case, during Mozafar al-Din Shah's trip to Austria and especially his stay in Vienna and Budapest, the ritual of receiving the Shah of Iran was accompanied by special and significant features, which are detailed here and based on the official documents of the Austrian government. And these will be discussed in the documentary anaylsis:

Vienna,

September 20, 1900.

On Thursday, September 20, 1900, at 5:45 p.m., the fifth king of the Qajar dynasty, with the delegation accompanying him, entered the Vienna railroad station, where he was received with great enthusiasm by the Austrian government. Vienna, the seat of the Austro-Hungarian monarchy, was the Shah's

233 As we said, Mozafar al din Shah, like his father, traveled to European countries 3 times and certainly saw very good theaters each time. But in this part, we will try to mention his trip to two very important cities in terms of theater and music at that time in Europe. It should be noted that all these documents, my personal findings, are from the document archives of the two mentioned countries.

first European destination after his trip to Russia, and Austrian government officials had prepared various programs to make the Shah of Iran's stay as pleasant and enjoyable as possible. This included taking the Iranian delegation to the Paré Theatre, which typically featured a more speechless performance, and often movement, dance, and music were the main elements of this type of show. However, after his escape from the Vienna train station, the Shah was escorted to the Hofburg Hotel, where he stayed under the official reception of political dignitaries and the Vienna police chief himself. The reception of the Shah of Iran was so formal and ostentatious that, on the orders of the Emperor of Austria, military marches were held on both sides of the road from Vienna's main train station to the hotel where he willingly stayed. A spectacular and coordinated military march that covered the continuous route. On the twentieth night, the Shah of Iran rests in the hotel to prepare for the exceptional events and programs of the following day. It is worth considering that giving to the custom and tradition of the city of music and art, Vienna's music performance was one of the inseparable elements of official ceremonies; and according to the nobles among the Austrian hosts, they tried to avoid any entertainment program and oriental language. The art intended for the king and his entourage should be in a way that is within the limits of Iranians' collective patience and comprehensibility.

Vienna,

September 21, 1900.

On Friday, after resting and doing some business, the king and his lieutenants prepared to participate in the dinner ceremony. According to the Shah, the ceremony was "elaboately decorated and magnificent." According to the plan, the gala dinner party was held at the Schönbrunn Palace in the presence of Emperor Franz Joseph I (1848-1916) and the accompanying political delegations, around five o'clock, and after the dinner, the high-ranking Austrian leaders were supposed to accompany the King of Iran to watch music and shows at Paré Theatre. The crucial point was that the emperor of Austria had prepared a partial display or a program of dance and singing combined with music and drama to pay utmost respect to the Shah of Iran and his entourage, and so as to make the program attractive and enjoyable for the Iranian delegation. But more importantly, there is no report of this side ceremony in Mozafar al din Shah's travelogue, and it can merely be learned by referring to Austrian government documents.

Document No. 55

Title of the Document:

Concert Program Presented in Honour of Mozaffar al-Din Shah at Schönbrunn Palace

Date: 21 September 1900

Repository:

Austrian State Archives, Vienna, Austria

Type of Document: Official Concert Program

Description of the Document:

This document contains the official musical program prepared for Mozaffar al-Din Shah during his stay in Vienna on 21 September 1900. Organized as part of the ceremonial festivities held in honour of the Persian monarch, the concert followed a gala reception and dinner attended by Emperor Franz Joseph I, members of the Austrian court, and representatives of both governments at Schönbrunn Palace.

The program includes a selection of orchestral and operatic compositions by prominent European composers, among them Ambroise Thomas, Charles Gounod, Giovanni Pierluigi da Palestrina, Alexander Zemlinsky, Jules Massenet, Johann Strauss, Ernst von Dohnányi and Gustav Mahler. The repertoire reflects the diversity of late nineteenth-century European musical culture and demonstrates the importance attached by the Austrian court to presenting its artistic achievements to distinguished foreign guests.

The significance of this document lies in its evidence of the cultural dimension of diplomatic relations between Qajar Iran and the Habsburg Empire. While Mozaffar al-Din Shah's travel memoirs contain little information regarding this particular event, Austrian archival records reveal the extent to which music, performance, and ceremonial spectacle were employed as instruments of royal hospitality. The concert formed part of a broader program designed to introduce the Persian monarch and his entourage to the artistic life of Vienna and to showcase the cultural prestige of the Austro-Hungarian Empire.

As a result, this document provides valuable insight into the role of music and court entertainment within the framework of international diplomacy at the turn of the twentieth century and illustrates how cultural performance functioned as a means of communication between European courts and visiting foreign rulers.

Source:

Austrian State Archives, Vienna. *Musik-Programm*, Schönbrunn Palace, 21 September 1900.

Fig. 55. Program of Concert visited of Mozafar al-Din Shah, Archive of Vienna, Austria, 1900.

At the dinner hosted by the emperor, apart from the heads and politicians of the Austrian government, the political figures of the Qajar government were present. Naturally, among the 25 men and political and service officials under Muzaffar al-Din Shah, such as: Amin al-Sultan, Hakim al-Mulk, Zahir al-Mulk, Mothaq al-Dawlah, Mofkham al-Dawlah, Mushir al-Mulk, and several other ministers, as well as people such as: Sani al-Sultaneh, the photographer, Nasser Homayoun, the chief of musicians. Especially, Nadim al-Sultan, the translator and a number of others, only 16 people were present in this ceremony.

After dinner, the Iranian delegation enjoyed the performance of the ballet show and music at Schönbrunn Palace. What was prepared for the Shah and his entourage in the Paré Theater was based on the knowledge of the Iranian group and their oriental taste. For this purpose, by looking at the Paré theater program, we can understand the element of movement is dance. Ballet Dramatic movements and. It can be perceived in most of these programs. Especially according to Document No. 5, it can be comprehended that Ballet, or dance, is included in most of Paré theater performances.

It is significant to consider the implementation of such artistic programs had an effect not only on the mind and spirit of Shah Qajar, but also on a number of cultured employees who were with him. Zahir al-Doulah was also present among the Iranian guests at the gala ceremony or the shows that took place in the Paré Theater.

The same person who had an active interest in the successful show and of course Ta'zieh, and in the performances of Ta'zieh in Takye Dawlat and other Tekyeh, mostly invited Western politicians to watch Ta'zieh. It is indeed claimed that he represents the author of the pieces that were displayed in his house under the title of Brotherhood.

Another prominent figure in common was Morteza Qoli Khan Sani al-Dawlah (1911-1857). A graduate of Dar al-Funun, who himself lived in Europe for a long time, and because of his familiarity with European languages like English and French, played a role in the discovery and expansion of the art of translation in the Qajar period. Ahmed Sani Al-Sultaneh, the director of Dar al-Funun Photo Gallery, too, was among the companions. The one who included his boy Mirza Ibrahim Khan, photographer Bashi, in the Shah's subsequent trip to Europe with him and among his presidential entourage, along with his father had a great impact on the art movement by printing the travelogue of the Shah and son, by taking numerous photos of the visited areas, which in turn affected the art of the Qajar period.

Vienna,

September 23, 1900.

Regarding Saturday, September 22 and the program of the Iranian delegation, the report of Mobarakeh's travelogue indicates that Shah Qajar, after watching the Vienna mosque and having lunch at the Iranian embassy in that city, went to a dinner at seven. The Crown Prince of Austria was invited and half an hour later, he sat down to attend the opera with the Emperor. An opera critic once described the Vienna Opera as "a game of intellect and ignorance." While it cannot be considered inferior to other opera houses, it does have certain advantages in some respects.

But at 9:30 am on September 23, Mozaffar al-Din Shah and his delegation went to a grassy area in the suburbs of Vienna to hunt. The hunting ceremony was tiring and naturally the Iranian delegation had of necessity to spend half the day resting in the hotel. But the entertainment program was sharply after six o'clock in the evening and, according to the previously arranged dinner, the Shah of Iran was the guest of the Emperor of Austria and a group of politicians from Vienna. At that time, which is to say at seven o'clock, the fireworks started.

A most impressive ritual for Iranians. Notably when they were mesmerized by the sound and lighting and were surprised to perceive the color of the sky. The ceremony was attended in one of the most beautiful parts of the Royal Schönbrunn Palace, located on the hill behind the very attractive and luxurious Gloritte building, and all the men who attended the ceremony had to wear formal attire complete with bow ties.

The fireworks began at seven o'clock with a very intense white light, and fifteen minutes later the white color gradually faded and was replaced by different colors, as if the sky was painted. Finally, at twenty-five minutes past seven, the fireworks on the hill reached their peak. It is interesting to note that in the report of Document 6, the exact location of the performers, the location of the floats, and the names of all the fireworks were accurately recorded.

Of course, earlier, that is, in August 1900 and during this first trip of Mozafar al din Shah, a music and fireworks ceremony was held at the Élysée Palace in France, which was accompanied by the initiative of the French hosts and the pleasure of the Shah, and even after listening to the music at the Paris exhibition, the Shah joyously ordered that harps be purchased.

Budapest.

24 September 1900.

The following destination was Budapest, the capital of Hungary. A country that joined Austria and formed the

Austro-Hungarian Empire. At 11:10 AM on Monday, September 24, 1900, Mozafar al-din Shah arrived in Budapest with his entourage by train from Vienna, and after the welcoming ceremony by Archduke Joseph August, the ruler of Hungary, and his entourage, he went to the Hungaria Hotel.

Regarding the hospitality program for this day of travel, there are two different accounts from two different documents. Documen ۵۷ , typically written in French by the European host several days before the king's arrival, contain at least four items that are somewhat suspicious. Would all these plans materialize after the appearance of the king or not?

Document No. 56

Title of the Document:

Official Carriage Arrangement Prepared for Mozaffar al-Din Shah's Arrival in Budapest

Date: 24 September 1900

Repository: Hungarian National Archives, Budapest, Hungary

Type of Document:

Official Ceremonial Planning Document

Description of the Document:

This document contains the official carriage arrangement prepared by the Hungarian authorities for the arrival of Mozaffar al-Din Shah in Budapest on 24 September 1900. Written in French prior to the Shah's arrival, it formed part of the hospitality program organized for the Persian monarch and his entourage during their visit to the Hungarian capital.

The document specifies the order of the carriages intended to transport the Shah, members of the Persian delegation, and Austro-Hungarian dignitaries from the railway station to the Hungaria Hotel following the official reception ceremony. It also records the names of several prominent Qajar officials accompanying the Shah, including Amin al-Sultan, Hakim al-Molk, Naser al-Molk, Zahir al-Dowleh, and other senior members of the royal entourage.

The importance of this document extends beyond its administrative function. Together with other documents relating to the Shah's stay in Budapest, it reveals the extent of the preparations undertaken by the host authorities before the arrival of the Persian monarch. As a planning document drafted several days in advance, it provides insight into the ceremonial expectations and logistical arrangements envisioned for the visit. At the same time, it raises an important historical question: whether all elements of the proposed program were ultimately carried out following the Shah's arrival, or whether some of the planned arrangements remained only on paper.

Consequently, the document offers valuable evidence for understanding the organization of Mozaffar al-Din Shah's European travels and the elaborate preparations made by Austro-Hungarian officials for the reception of a visiting foreign ruler at the turn of the twentieth century.

Source:

Hungarian National Archives, Budapest. *Rangement des voitures pour le trajet de la gare de l'ouest à l'hôtel Hungaria*, 24 September 1900.

Fig. 56. List of companions of Mozafar al-Din Shah in Budapest, Archive of Vienna, Austria, September 1900.

1. All the verbs are expressed in the future tense and it is clear that arrangements were planned before the arrival of the Iranian group and by the executive officials in Budapest for the arrival of the Shah, from appointments to clogging the streets for the Iranian delegation.

2. The visible presence of red and blue crosses in the document reinforces the possibility that some of these programs have been removed or completely changed.

3. Document 8 shows that on the same day, the Shah went to attend an opera with an oriental style and content, an opera for which correspondence had been done a long time ago. Despite such contradictions, it is possible all the events of these events transpired.

Document No. 57

Title of the Document:

Detailed Program of Mozaffar al-Din Shah's Visit to Budapest

Date: September 1900

Repository: Austrian State Archives, Vienna, Austria

Type of Document:

Official Ceremonial and Hospitality Program

Description of the Document:

This document contains a detailed program prepared for Mozaffar al-Din Shah's visit to Budapest in September 1900. Written in French prior to the arrival of the Persian monarch, it outlines a series of official visits, receptions, inspections, and public appearances planned by the Hungarian authorities during the Shah's stay in the city.

The program provides a rare glimpse into the extensive preparations undertaken by the hosts before the arrival of the Persian delegation. The use of future-tense verbs throughout the document clearly indicates that it was drafted as a proposed schedule rather than a record of completed events. The itinerary includes visits to public institutions, ceremonial meetings with local officials, and appearances at important urban landmarks, reflecting the organizers' intention to present Budapest as a modern and prosperous European capital.

Particularly noteworthy are the handwritten annotations, markings, and corrections visible throughout the document. These additions suggest that the original program was revised during the course of the visit and raise the possibility that some of the proposed activities were altered, postponed, or cancelled. When examined alongside other contemporary documents relating to the Shah's stay in Budapest, the program highlights the distinction between official planning and the actual course of events.

The importance of this document therefore lies not only in the information it provides about the intended reception of Mozaffar al-Din Shah, but also in the insight it offers into the practical realities of organizing a royal visit at the turn of the twentieth century. It illustrates the degree of preparation undertaken by the host authorities while simultaneously revealing traces of adjustment and negotiation that accompanied the implementation of the ceremonial program.

Source:

Austrian State Archives, Vienna. *Programme détaillé de la visite de quelques édifices et institutions publiques de Budapest, à présenter à Sa Majesté le Shah de la Perse*, September 1900.

Fig. 57. Program of Mozafar al-Din Shah's visit to Budapest, Archive of Vienna, Austria, September 1900.

Budapest

25 September, 1900.

What the twenty-fitth document narrates contains very useful information that includes important and key points from a show point of view.

> I am pleased to inform you that the Shah of Persia will arrive on the 25th of the 8th month at 7 ½ am to participate in the gala evening organized in his honor, and I ask you to represent the ballet *Zulejka* in three acts and the first act of the opera *Queen of Sheba*. I also ask you to ensure that the duration of the entire show does not exceed two (2) hours and not to start it before Your Majesty the Shah has arrived. The Shah and his party will be seated through the separate entrance.

Document No. 58

Title of the Document:

Official Correspondence Concerning Mozaffar al-Din Shah's Attendance at the Budapest Opera

Date: 25 September 1900

Repository: Hungarian National Archives, Budapest, Hungary

Type of Document:

Official Administrative Correspondence

Description of the Document:

This document consists of an official communication issued in preparation for Mozaffar al-Din Shah's attendance at a gala performance in Budapest on 25 September 1900. Addressed to the responsible authorities of the opera house, the letter outlines the artistic program that was to be presented in honour of the Persian monarch and his entourage.

According to the document, the organizers were instructed to perform the ballet *Zulejka* in three acts together with the first act of Karl Goldmark's opera *The Queen of Sheba*. The correspondence further specifies that the entire performance should not exceed two hours and that the program was not to begin before the arrival of the Shah. It also records that a separate entrance had been arranged for the Persian ruler and his party, reflecting the ceremonial considerations associated with the visit.

The importance of this document lies in the insight it provides into the careful planning undertaken by Hungarian authorities before the Shah's arrival. Unlike general hospitality schedules, this correspondence relates directly to a specific theatrical event and demonstrates the extent to which artistic performances formed an integral part of the official reception organized for the Persian monarch. Particularly noteworthy is the selection of *Zulejka* and *The Queen of Sheba*, both works drawing upon themes associated with the Orient, suggesting a deliberate effort to present productions that would appeal to the distinguished guest from Persia.

Examined alongside other documents relating to Mozaffar al-Din Shah's stay in Budapest, this correspondence offers valuable evidence of the role played by opera and ballet in the cultural diplomacy of the Austro-Hungarian Empire at the beginning of the twentieth century.

Source:

Hungarian National Archives, Budapest. Official correspondence concerning the gala performance organized for Mozaffar al-Din Shah, 25 September 1900.

Fig. 58. Report on the presence of Mozafar al-Din Shah in the Budapest opera, Archive of Budapest.

Budapest,

September 26, 1900.

At 9 o'clock in the morning the Shah left the hotel and went to visit the Budapest Arms Factory. He was accompanied by Hungary's Minister of Trade during this visit. At that time, which is to say at 11:30, he went to the National Museum and Art Collection of Budapest and was greeted by the Minister of Culture and the director of the National Museum. At 2:00 p.m., after a tour of Marguerite Island, the king returned to the hotel. According to the documents, all the passageways of the king of Iran were blocked for ordinary people, and it was impossible to pass through.

Also, granting to the documents, moving to Franz Joseph Square located on Academia Street to identify the new building of the Hungarian Parliament and meeting with a number of politicians, including the Minister of Trade of Hungary, was one of Mozaffar ad-Din Shah's other plans. At this place, the king was greeted very formally and warmly. The executive director of Hungary approached the Shah of Iran to confront him and accompanied him on his journey. Then, accompanied by dignitaries, Gisela train station and Budapest Zoo metro station were visited. The visit was conducted completely by train, but there is no mention of it in Mobarakeh's travelogue.

According to the available documents, all the visitors were placed in four vehicles, and the description goes beyond stating just this. At the station, the Shah and others enjoyed exploring several museums, especially the Trade and Communication Museum, until noon, when the Iranian guests returned to the Hungarian Hotel. Around 3:00 PM, the Shah decided to take a stroll through the streets of Budapest accompanied by the Chief of Ceremonies of the

Hungarian Government. They planned to return to the hotel at 5:00 PM.

Budapest,

September 27, 1900.

Finally, it was time to flee and at 10:30 a.m. on Thursday, the 27th of September 1900, with the warm welcome of the ruler of Hungary and high-ranking Hungarian officials, and amidst the uproar of the chants of "Long live the king!" of the people of Budapest, Mozafar al-Din Shah Qajar left Hungary for Serbia and the Ottoman borders.

It is certain that the kings and other Qajar political dignitaries sat down to watch the theatre and opera in other trips to Europe and wrote down their observations as they thought. But what was said above was part of the experience of watching the European theatre of Naser al Din Shah and Mozafar al Din Shah during their first trip to Europe. Narrations that were sometimes accompanied by contradictions. Anyway, one of the ways that Iranians got to know European shows was through these trips, some of which were documented.

2. Consulates

Nowadays, embassies and consulates of friendly countries have a permanent presence and activity in the capital and major cities of every country. The employees of each embassy also enjoy the hospitality of the host country. And within the framework of certain international regulations, they are responsible for regulating relations and protecting the interests of their country, and one of their tasks is to collect the necessary information from all aspects and issues of the country where they are assigned and provide it to their governments.

But in the past centuries, this was not the case, although when necessary, the kingdom would send an ambassador to the court of another king to carry out a certain mission, which was mostly to deliver letters. The establishment of permanent embassies in Europe became common since the end of the seventeenth century, and in Iran, as all fundamental reforms begin with the name of Amir Kabir, he established the first permanent embassies of Iran in the last years of his chancellorship in 1850 in London and St. Petersburg.

On the other hand, from the reign of Shah Abbas onwards, representatives from various lands came to Iran and the Shah's court with different titles. Most of them were representatives of their governments who came to this land for alliances and political, commercial, and other treaties, at a time when Westerners' curiosity about the East, particularly Iran, was at its peak.

They came, found, saw, wrote, and took away. Each and every one of these travelers extensively collected materials from all the ceremonies that were prepared for them. They documented everything they desired from Iranian culture through the medium of the diary. The most interesting thing is that today, we use their memories of Iran as documentary sources.[234]

---

[234]To avoid any repetition, I simply mention the names of these individuals. However, conducting research on the works and activities of these elders is a topic that is beyond the scope of this article.

Among the important European travelers, names such as Pietro Della Valle, Adam Olarios, Figueroa, Michele Membre, and Tavarnier can be mentioned. They have repeatedly mentioned Iranian theatrical forms and small plays in their observations of Iran during the Safavid period.

But in the Qajar period, these visits continued, even more so than during the Safavid period. The visitors came to Iran for various purposes, including commercial ventures, political treaties, and teaching at Dar al-Funun. Among them, there were those who traveled out of personal curiosity and documented their observations.

It was during the reign of Fath Ali Shah that official diplomatic relations began in Iran. There were no permanent embassies located in the center of government. There were no fixed or permanent ambassadors in Iran. And sometimes, when foreign ambassadors and representatives entered the capital, they would first present their gifts and letters to the Shah of Iran before leaving the court on receiving a response.[235]

Little by little, with the arrival of Naser al-Din Shah, permanent ambassadors came to Iran. Among the foreign governments, Russia, England, and France surpassed other countries in their involvement with Iran.

When every other country established its permanent base in Iran, their employees gradually brought their families and associates. Each community had its own artists and shows to provide entertainment for their families. Sometimes guests were invited to these shows,[236] and occasionally foreigners were invited to watch Iranian performances. From the above

---

[235]Peter Avari, *History of Iran,translator Morteza Sghebfar, (Afshar Zand Qajar)*, 313

point, it can be said that these show invitations could have a lot of influence over time.

A clear example of these invitations can be mentioned in the handwritten Document 5٩ dated May 1905, in which it is explained how it was the custom of the people of Fars that on one of the first ten days of the month of Muharram, the families of foreign ambassadors were invited to participate in the Ta'zia. They knew how interested they are and how much they like to know and see Iranian Theatre.

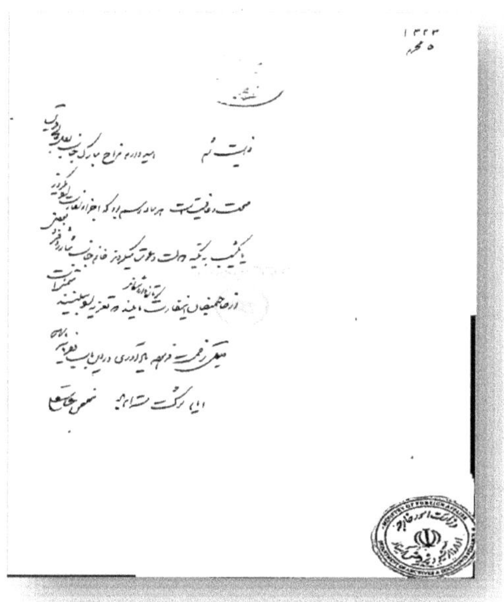

Fig. 59. Handwritten Invitation to the families of foreign governments to see ta'ziyah, Tehran Ministry of Foreign Affairs document archive, 1905.

3. Armenian communities

When the Armenians lost their independence, Armenia became, for a certain period, a no-man's land between the

Persians and the Ottomans,[237] where for some years the former ruled and, for others, we witnessed the domination of the latter. During the seventeenth century Armenian territory was under the control of the Turks.[238]

During this Ottoman rule, the Armenians found themselves experiencing many difficulties due to the tyranny that the Turks exercised over the population: between a very high tax system (those who did not pay would have faced death) and between persecutions linked to religious causes (the Turks professed Islam while the Armenians were Christians) the daily life of the Armenians became truly unsustainable.

In that same period, Shah Abbas I reined in Persia, and he wanted to attack Armenia because he longed to avenge his ancestors' defeat at the hands of the Turks and because he hoped for the help of the local population for an easy conquest. In fact, until then, the Shah had welcomed many Armenians who fled their homeland into Persia and knew that, not being able to have their own independence, the Armenians would have preferred the Persian presence to the Turkish one.[239]

If we add to this that the Turkish dominion had also extended to the Persian city of Tabriz (a politically and geographically crucial point), we understand how the Persian sovereign needed no further reasons to go to war against the

---

237 Wars began in the sixteenth century under the leadership of Shah Isma'il Safavi, the founder of the Safavid dynasty of Persia and the Ottoman kingdom of Sultan Salim. The importance of these wars lies in the fact that Persia was the only center of the Shia religions while the Ottoman Empire was the center of the Sunni religion. Clashes between these two empires were most common in the regions of Eastern Anatolia, the Middle East and the Caucasus. These wars were continued after the Safavid Empire by the Afsharid and Zande Qajar governments.

238 Haroton Drhohanian, translator Leon Minasian, *History of Jolfa of Isfahan*, [Tārīkh-i Julfā-yi Iṣfahān](Isfahan Zende Rud, 2000), 1-3.

239 Ibid 9-12.

Ottomans. The Shah first decided to attack Tabriz without warning, playing on the factor of surprise which earned him the conquest of the city, after which he turned north towards Armenia. Before reaching Armenia, in the Sofian[240] desert, the Persian army came into contact with the Ottoman army of Ali Pàscia:[241] a clear Persian victory ensued which helped to create a demoralizing psychological factor in the Turkish army against the army of Shah Abbas II. From this victory onwards, the Persians encountered no difficulty in entering Armenia, where the welcome that the local population reserved for the Shah when he entered the cities was noteworthy: they ordered processions with leafy branches and, throwing petals as he passed, praised him and Persia.[242]

The event is narrated in the history of Arakel[243] by Arakel of Tabriz, an Armenian historian of that era.

The entry of the Persians into Armenia led to the withdrawal of the Ottomans to a fortress near Iravan. This decision to take refuge in the castle was useless, as the Persian army managed to conquer it, obtaining another important victory.

However, the Shah wanted to show great humanity by proposing to the defeated the option to remain in those territories (now Persian) if they wanted: some preferred to leave Armenia to return to the West and others remained in those lands.[244]

Around 1603, fearing that the sultan might decide to reconquer Armenia and take revenge on the local population, guilty of having helped the Persians drive out the Turks, the

---

[240] A Persian city in eastern Azerbaijan.

[241] (1519 – 1587) Ottoman privateer and admiral.

[242] Haroton Drhohanian, translator Leon, Minasian, *History of Jolfa of Isfahan*, [Tārīkh-i Julfā-yi Iṣfahān], (Isfahan, Zendeh Rood, 2000), 4-7.

[243] Arakel Davrizhetsi, edited by L.A. Khanlarian, *Story of Arakel*, (Iravan, Academy of Science of Armenia and Russia, 1990).

[244] Haroton Drhohanian, translator Leon Minasian, *History of Jolfa of Isfahan*, [Tārīkh-i Julfā-yi Iṣfahān] 9-11.

Shah decided to move the Armenian people to Persia, destroying all the cities and crops to discourage and embarrass the Ottoman troops.[245]

This act was not only due to the humanity and compassion of the Persian ruler; in fact, knowing that his own country was not in a good economic situation, he welcomed the integration of the Armenians in Persia, given their mercantile ability. Thus it was that Tahmaseb Gholi Beik, by order of the Shah, moved the Armenians to Persia; the migration process took place in three waves and the last occurred when the Armenian population of Jolfa (the last inhabited city of Armenia) left for Tehran and other cities such as Kashan, Rasht, Anzali and Isfahan.[246]

It must be said that it is possible to find in Persia a city named Jolfa founded by the newly arrived Armenians in honor of their ancient home. The stable and, by now, established Armenian presence gave way to a very important process of cultural integration: Persian culture, in every aspect (artistic, religious, social), was renewed thanks to the knowledge of the Armenian people who, as already stated, had excelled in the art of commerce.

Precisely because of their ability, the ruler of Persia decided to send these merchants everywhere on behalf of Persia; from China to Europe, not forgetting India and Egypt, all in search of beneficial trade. Particularly important in Europe was the city of Venice, where several businessmen were sent who found in the Serenissima an environment suitable for very important exchanges and agreements. Contacts with the Venetian world can also be perceived from an artistic point of view where, by now consolidated trade routes, allowed artists of all fields to travel to get to know new cultures.

---

[245] Ibid 5-8.

[246] Haroton Drhohanian, translator Leon Minasian, *History of Jolfa of Isfahan*, [Tārīkh-i Julfā-yi Iṣfahān], 18-22.

Among these artists, Minas deserves special mention, a painter of whom there is no certain data except that he lived in the seventeenth century.[247]

Being in contact with the Venetian world and, more generally, with Italian artistic culture, he got to know Western painting with all its styles and canons and, on returning to Persia, painted various works that were clearly influenced by the Italian style.[248]

Also according to what Arakel writes in his work,[249] one day the Shah, after seeing a fresco of Minas, was so admiring of it that he decided to invite the artist to court to propose that he become his personal painter. It is not known exactly how things went, but what is certain is that shortly thereafter the young Armenian Minas worked on the royal palace on behalf of the sovereign. The most important works of Minas are found in the church of Vank,[250] where several frescoes were made in clear Italian style. It is fascinating to note how the exterior of the church is influenced by Persian architecture, to the point of looking more like a mosque than a church. The interior, on the other hand, seems to catapult the visitor directly to Italy due to the style of decoration used.[251]

Echmiadzin Cathedral and Vank Church

As we have already mentioned, the Armenians were transferred to Persia after the Persian army conquered Armenia. Thousands and thousands started this diaspora in

---

[247] William Bayne Fisher, translator Yaghub Azhand, *History of the Safavids*, 244-247.

[248] Mania Ghazarian, translator Edik Baghdasarian, *The paintings of new Jolfa of Isfahan*, Hovik (Tehran, Ogharian, 1984), 23.

[249] Arakel Davrizhetsi, edited by L.A. Khanlarian, *Story of Arakel*, 324-325

[250] Church of Armenians in Isfahan. It was founded in 1655.

[251] Haroton Drhohanian, translator Leon Minasian, *History of Jolfa of Isfahan*, [Tārīkh-i Julfā-yi Iṣfahān], 30-36.

the Iranian territory and in its cities. Among these, Isfahan deserves a special mention as it probably hosted the highest number of Armenians.

When the Shah conquered Armenia, he ordered the destruction of all buildings. However, he faced significant resistance from the local population when he attempted to tear down the cathedral of Echmiadzin, which was considered a place of immense sacredness. In the end the Persian ruler, wanting to leave only scorched earth to the Turks if they returned, decided to transport this extraordinary place of worship to Persia, partially disassembling it (some columns, stones and epigraphs) and then reassembling it in Isfahan; this fact also contributed to the presence of a large number of Armenian settlers in this Persian city. Over the years the Armenian community, transplanted in the heart of the city, progressed and grew more and more; this allowed the priests and the population to ask the ruler of Persia to be able to enlarge their church (the so-called church of Vank), which, with royal permission, was renovated in 1654 and since then it has become a place of worship, as well as artistically very important. It must be said that a merit of the Shah was to allow the Armenians to freely profess their beliefs. This aspect should not be underestimated because in the Islamic world of the seventeenth century, this "license" was an absolute novelty and, naturally, not by everyone, especially the most extremists, was it seen with a good eye.[252]

The architecture of this church is truly unique in the world as it represents a fusion of seventeenth century Safavid-Islamic art and Armenian-Christian style. At the main entrance there is a large door that opens onto the internal courtyard in which the bell tower stands out majestically, which was built about forty years after 1654. The interior of this extraordinary building, on the other hand, presents, thanks to the superb work of Minas, frescoes that are strongly affected by

252 Ibid 60-61.

Fig.60. Wall paintings of the Vank church, Isfahan.

the Italian influence, to such an extent that we can speak of an Armenian-Italian style. The most majestic ones depict the Last Supper, the Birth of Jesus and the Crucifixion.[253]

Another relevant aspect of Armenian society given by the large presence of books that the Armenians had brought with them during their emigration to Persia; they dealt with topics of all kinds and, probably, constituted the true cultural treasure, as well as the legacy and identity of the Armenian civilization. The Armenian archbishop Khachatur Kesaratsi,[254] aware of this richness, decided to reproduce these important (and requested) writings in more recent versions; from this came the first reprint of these works which inevitably ended up infecting Persian art and culture as well. The work was possible thanks to Kesaratsi sending two men to Europe (Italy and Amsterdam to be exact) to import, in 1647, the science of printing conceived two centuries

[253] Ibid 387.

[254] He was an archbishop in the Safavid Empire of ethnic Armenians. He is credited with inventing the first printing press in Persia, in 1633 or 1636.

earlier by Johann Gutenberg; thanks to them we have the first printing press in Persia.

The presence of the press and the importation, as well as that of goods, of books by Armenian merchants sent all over the world allowed the translation into Armenian and the printing of works on any subject: from philosophy to geography, from history to theatre. Precisely that of the theater proved to be an aspect of particular interest for Armenian culture and subsequently for Persian culture, which found itself absorbing the knowledge that Armenians learned from all over the world.[255] An incredibly valid and important source for knowledge of Armenian culture is the Prayer Book,[256] written in 1687, wherein religious-theatrical customs are explored. The very interesting aspect of this work is that the setting of the same seems to follow the canons of a screenplay: there are parts written in black that represent the words, the dialogues or the rites that the priest recites, while it is possible to find in red the indications that the prelate and/or the assembly must follow.

---

255 William Bayne Fisher, translator Yaghub Azhand, *History of the Safavids*, 244.

256 Prayer book is kept in Isfahan in the Vank church museum.

Fig. 61. Book of Prayers, Vank Church, Isfahan, 1687.

4. Tekyeh Dowlat

Tekie Dowlat,[257] Tekie Homayoni,[258] Tekie Gasr,[259] Tekie Bozorge Shahi:[260] these are the names of a large theater built in the Qajar period. We have no documents that provide useful information on the period in which the building was built, but it is presumable that the work was started after the European travels of King Naser al-Din Shah. According to some scholars, such as Bahram Beyzaee and Yahya Zoka,[261] referring to the most characteristic aspects of the ancient Persian squares and caravanserais, however, the palace would have already existed before the Shah's European trips.

However, the hypothesis, if not of the construction, of modernization of this building following the trips to Europe

---

257 Mohammad Moein, *Persian dictionary*, Farhang-i Fārsī, 1122.Tekie of government.

258 Ibid 3574. Royal Tekie

259 Ibid 1836. Castle Tekie.

260 Ibid 418. Royal big tekie.

261 Authoritative Iranian historian and Persian art historian (1923-2000).

made by Naser al-Din Shah remains plausible. After his first visit to Europe in 1873, the king then traveled to Italy, Austria, England, France, and other countries, remaining impressed and fascinated by European theatres: hence his intention to have a similar one in his capital of his kingdom.

As we have already mentioned, the king made three trips to various countries in Europe. As is customary, in every situation, the protocol required at least one evening at the opera, a concert, or a prose theatrical performance. It is only after these trips that the king learns to appreciate entertainment in its various forms, an interest that he had not previously shown in his country. Through this experience, he comes to understand how music and entertainment are also crucial for European rulers, both from a cultural and political perspective. This resulted in a change in his judgment of artists, actors, and musicians.

Fig. 62. Dowlat Theater under construction, Golestan Place, Qajar period.

Documents show that the king attended, among others, musical performances at the Royal Albert Hall in London, but that he was particularly impressed by a show in a Parisian theater whose name is not mentioned: it is known that it was six floors, with sumptuous stages, and above all with beautiful actresses from Paris or Canada. Subsequent trips see him in Vienna, where one of the most important performances he attends is in Redouten Salen.[262]

Tekie of Dowlat was located southwest of Golestan Castle and southeast of Shamsolemare (a courtyard that Nasser al-Din Shah had built before his three voyages). It was a three-story structure with a circular plan, built entirely of bricks, with a diameter of about sixty meters and a height of about twenty-four. In the middle of the ground floor was a circular space, which was used for Ta'ziyah performances.

During the construction of the Dowlat palace, several people (aristocrats and non-aristocrats) criticized the king for this construction, as they accused the sovereign of being too sympathetic to Europeans. Only later, once the construction was completed, did the criticism cease and, on the contrary, the importance of this structure was recognized, especially by the religious who saw the palace as an excellent space to be able to give life to religious performances. The Dowlat Theatre was very similar to the Royal Albert Hall in London and was the symbol of the Qajar government of that period. It was the first building of this size. The year in which it was built is not known, but it is thought to have been built approximately between 1863 and 1868. The head of the construction works was Dust Ali Khan,[263] although scholars believe that the architect was Hossein Ali Mehr Bon[264] who

262 Naser al din Shah Qajar, edited by Fatemeh Ghazi ha, *Diary of Naser al-Din Shah,* [Rūznāmah-'i khāṭirāt-i Nāṣir al-Dīn Shāh], (Tehran, Research Office of the National Documents Organization of Iran , 1993), 217-220.

263 Moayer ol mamalek or Nezam ol doleh architect active during the reign of Naser al din Shah (1820-1875).

264 Mohamad Ali pir Niaka in his book Persian Architecture. Honar Eslami, Tehran, 2002, says that the architect was probably Hossein Ali Mehr Bon, on whose life there is not much information.

had already distinguished himself in the past for his great ability to build important buildings.[265]

Fig. 63. Men's auditorium at Tekyeh Dowlat, Golestan Place, Qajar period.

Yahia Zoka, the Persian writer, in his work on the history of the castle of Golestan, states that the construction of the Dowlat Theatre was born from the need to contain many more people than in previous theatres, where space shortages were enormous. The new construction also allowed women to participate in the shows, having their own space.[266]

---

265 Mohamad Karim Pir nia, *the form of the architecture of Iran*, Tehran , Islamic Art, 2002), 145.

266 Yahya Zoka, *History of Golestan Castle*,[Tārīkhchah-i sākhtimānhā-yi Arg-i Salṭanatī-i Tihrān : va rāhnamā-yi Kākh-i Gulistān], (Tehran Anjoman asar Meli, 1970), 88.

The surface on which the theatre was built was circular and occupied 2,824 square meters; the building had a height of twenty-four meters and a diameter of sixty meters.[267]

The structure was divided into three floors, plus an underground floor. It had an octagonal shape and was constructed entirely of white bricks, adorned with various Persian patterns. The dome of the building was constructed using wood, with reinforced points made of iron. Additionally, a large cloth could be used to provide further protection in case of rain or snow. Subsequently, some of the wooden beams gave way, which is why a team of French engineers did their utmost to replace them with pieces entirely in iron. Furthermore, due to the size of the building, its weight was not adequately supported by the load-bearing beams. The was the reason why the top floor (the fourth) was eliminated and the beams were also replaced with iron bars.[268]

This theatre had three doors. The main door had an entrance facing east and, for religious reasons, was reserved for men only. This door was built in wood and had the typology of the pointed arch. The second door also had a pointed arch shape, but the entrance was oriented to the east, and was reserved for women only. Above this gate were six minarets.[269]

---

[267] Mohamad Hasan Khan Etemad ol saltaneh, *Al-Moaser Al-Asar, in forty years of Iranian history*, (Tehran Asatir, 1984) , p.87.
[268] Mostafa Oskuee, *History of Iranian Theater*,[Pizhūhishī dar tārīkh-i ti'ātr-i Īran], (Tehran, Anahita, 1992), 79-80
[269] Mohamad Hasan Khan Etemad ol saltaneh, *Al-Moaser Al-Asar, in forty years of Iranian history*, 87.

Fig. 64. Women's auditorium at Tekyeh Dowlat, Golestan Place, Qajar period.

The third and last door was reserved for members of the royal family. Once passed, you entered a corridor that led to the Royal Box: this was built on two floors and was composed of a canopy supported by many columns which in turn formed twenty small arches. The columns were of hand-made pottery with imaginative motifs, in gold and silver that chased each other.[270]

In the Royal Part of the theatre, there was a sort of curtain that allowed the king to watch the show perfectly but without being seen by the people.[271] If one of the people dared to turn his gaze to look at the king's face, he would be sentenced to death. The nobles and ministers of the king also lived on the first floor, but obviously their wives, even noble ones, were not allowed to stay with them. On the second floor it was possible to find women (aristocrats), while on the

---

270 Carla Serena, translator Golamreza Samee, *Iran's people and sights*, Mardum va dīdanīhā-yi Īrān : safar'nāmah, 162.

271 Yahya Zoka, *History of Golestan Castle*, [Tārīkhchah-i sākhtimānhā-yi Arg-i Salṭanatī-i Tihrān : va rāhnamā-yi Kākh-i Gulistān], 297.

third and last floor there were the Nagarechi, who were the musicians.[272]

As previously mentioned, the theater had a circular shape with the stage positioned in the center. Those who viewed the stage from behind were typically lower-class individuals, some of whom stood on the ground floor. Obviously, even here, the presence of women was not anticipated. In fact, it must be said that the presence of women, even though they were aristocrats and sometimes even the wives of the king, caused quite a few embarrassments. That is why the doors of the women's boxes had curtains that prevented others from noticing their presence. Furthermore, and always on the same floor, as well as on the first floor, the floors were adorned with sublime hand-embroidered Persian carpets (also made of silk for the king).

Both on the external walls and inside the structure, it was possible to find a significant presence of candelabra. However, the central and primary lighting came from an imposing chandelier, which presumably had a diameter of at least five meters. In those rare cases where more light was needed, small bulbs were used.[273]

The stage had a circular shape, with a diameter of nine meters and a height of ninety centimetres. The border was adorned with sumptuous marble, while the inside of the stage was made entirely of brick. Within this area there were spaces for the actors who, without being seen by the audience, could watch the opera during the scenes in which they were not acting. To get on stage, two ladders built on opposite edges of the stage were used. Around the stage there was a circular space, about six meters in diameter, where animals (mostly

[272] Mostafa Oskuee, *History of Iranian Theater*, [Pizhūhishī dar tārīkh-i ti'ātr-i Īran], 80.
[273] Abd allah Mostofi, *Explaining of My life*, Sharḥ-i zindagānī-i man, yā, Tārīkh-i ijtimāʿī va idārī-i dawrah-i Qājārīyah ,296.

horses) passed through. A little beyond this circular space was the area dedicated to the lower classes of society.[274]

It was slightly raised in order to allow the spectators residing therein a better vision. This space could hold up to a maximum of five thousand people.

Minbar is a type of chair in which the Sheykh or a person who wanted to narrate some religious topic, such as the lives of saints, sat.

In the Dowlat Theatre there was a minbar with about twenty steps and it was built of marble. A sheik climbed onto it and spoke to everyone about the situation in Kerbela.[275]

Naser al-Din Shah gave the order to build the theatre. However, this directive, according to some sources, would have taken place even before he made his travels in Europe; this was said in reply to those who insinuated that the theatre was built according to European design. Naser al Din Shah thus claimed authorship of the style of the monument entirely for him, attributing it solely and exclusively to Persian culture and architecture.

The director of the Dowlat Theatre was Moin Al Boka,[276] but at the same time he was a very good musician, a very good director, and a superb actor. He chose the actors and organized the scenes. The king of Persia Naser al Din Shah ordered Mirza Nasrollah Esfahani to collect the ancient

---

274 Yahya Zoka and Mohamad Hasan Semsar, *Tehran in pictures*, [Tihrān dar taṣvīr], (Tehran, Sorosh, 1980), second volume, 3-6.

275 Yahya Zoka, History of Golestan Castle, [Tārīkhchah-i sākhtimānhā-yi Arg-i Salṭanatī-i Tihrān : va rāhnamā-yi Kākh-i Gulistān], 297.

276 Mohammad Hasan khan Etemad ol Saltaneh, edited by Iraj Afshar *The Diary of Etemad ol Saltaneh*, [Rūznāmah-'i khāṭirāt-i I'timād al-Salṭanah], Amir Kabir, Tehran, 1966).

poetic texts of the Ta'ziyah and to collaborate with Moin Al Boka to stage them.[277]

The theatre also had a funerary function, as in the time of Mozaffar al-Din Shah (1896-1907), whose funeral ceremony was celebrated inside the Dowlat, accompanied by many Nohe (typical Persian funeral songs), where the crowd mourned the deceased sovereign with heartrending and very heated lamentations.[278]

Subsequently, after the expulsion of Mohammad ʿAli Shah (1909), the theatrical genre of Ta'ziyah, like all religious ones on the other hand, disappeared from the Dowlat Theatre. Furthermore, by now, the theatre with all its glories was seen more and more as a place where political rather than theatrical activity could be carried out.

The Dowlat Theatre was a symbol of the Tehran government, and it was a source of personal pride and identification.[279] Paradoxically it was destroyed in 1946 in order to build a bank.

Today, the peculiarities of the Dowlat Theatre are known thanks to Mohammad Ghaffari (1845-1940), better known as Kamal-ol-Molk, a famous Iranian painter from the Ghaffari family of Kashan. He wrote in his diary all the details of the theater and thanks to it, it is now possible to reconstruct the theatre exactly as it was.

5. Dar al Fonun's Theatre

277 Abd allah Mostofi, *Explaining of My life*, [Sharḥ-i zindagānī-i man, yā, Tārīkh-i ijtimāʿī va idārī-i dawrah-i Qājārīyah], 308.

278 Mohamad Ali Katuzian Tehrani, *Analysis and Research on the Persian Constitutional Revolution*, [Mushāhidāt va taḥlīl-i ijtimāʿī va siyāsī az tārīkh-i inqilāb-i mashrụṭīyat-i Īrān Enteshar], (Tehran, Intishar, 2000), 417.

279 Carla Serena, translator Golamreza Samee, *Iran's people and sights*, [Mardum va dīdanīhā-yi Īrān: safar'nāmah], 242.

After making his travels in Europe and admiring some of the theatre buildings he visited, the king of Persia, Naser al-Din Shah returned to his homeland and ordered the construction of a theatre palace specifically for the representation of comedies and musical works. The Dar al Fonun Theatre with a French plan was built in 1877 under the direction of Ali Akbar Khan Mozaian al Dole and had a capacity of three hundred spectators.[280]

The first Persian interpreters who performed in this theater building had no knowledge of European theatre; therefore, they needed the teachings of European artists who went to Persia. The director and set designer of the theatre, Mozaian al Dole, wanted the actors to act just like that.

The great Persian writer Rashid Yasemi,[281] in his history of Persian literature says:

> King Naser al din Shah, after his travels in Europe, and after appreciating the European spectacular forms, ordered Mozaian al Dole to set up shows in the European manner. Therefore, Mozaian al Dole can be considered the first person who staged plays with a different style than those produced up to then in Persia (Ta'ziyah and Taghlid). Among these were some performances by Molière, which at that time were among the few accepted by the people.

Hassan Shirvani (1895- 1951 Tehran) recalls that "Mozaian al Dole in collaboration with other famous comic actors, such as Karim Shiree and Esmail Bazaz, created shows such as Molière's *Le Mariage forcé*. The actors did not act according to

[280] Fereidun Adamiat, *Amir kabir and Iran*, [Amīr Kabīr va Īrān], (Tehran, Kharazmi, 1977), 367.
[281] Persian translator and historian.

the script but through the knowledge of the text they tried to improvise."[282]

The performances were usually of French classics, in Persian translation, and mainly by Molière. The ruling class did not look kindly on them, especially for their content, which was deemed unsuitable for the population.[283] Probably society itself was not yet prepared for this kind of show and it would take some time before it was accepted and appreciated.

Later, comedians also arrived from Europe who collaborated with Persian actors in Persian comedies, much appreciated by an audience that appreciated the mix between European and local theatre; thus a new kind of show was born which had the structure of Persian theatre but with strong European influences.

The basic theatrical text was the French one, modified and adapted according to Persian customs, marked by improvisation, with the actors who stuffed their acting with the most characteristic jokes of their culture, making it more familiar and well accepted by spectators.[284]

6. The translation industry

With the reign of Fath Ali Shah communications between Persia and France begin to thicken more than those with Russia and England. There are various reasons, but it must be emphasized that it was precisely through these exchanges that a more specific knowledge of theatrical terminology spread in

282 Hassan Shirvani, *Artistic Activities in 50 Years of the Pahlavi Empire*, (Tehran, Vezarat Farhang va Honar, 1971), 27.
283 Mostafa Oskuee, *History of Iranian Theater*, [Pizhūhishī dar tārīkh-i ti'ātr-i Īran], 160-161.
284 Niyayesh Pur Hassan, *(Dar ol Fonun)*, [Jaryān-i.talīʻah-'i tiyātr dar Īrān va sarguzasht-i tamāshākhānah-'i Dār al-Funūn[, (Tehran, Kule poshti 2017), 168-169.

Persia, due also to the diffusion of famous writers and theatrical authors.

We have already said how much the Persian theatrical show underwent changes after the experiences of the students sent abroad (France, Russia and England). Thanks to these experiences, not only the theatrical tradition of these countries entered Persia, but also their literature. It has also been shown that King Nasser al-Din Shah made three important trips to Europe and that these influenced the theatre of that period.

The Renaissance also initiates a new humanistic vision in France, placing it among the countries that are distinguished by a form of civilization that is detached from the medieval one, at the same time assuming the role of a leading nation in language and culture. In addition to princes, writers and scholars also tried to learn the language, conforming to the new culture. Persia, since the Safavid period, began to communicate with France and probably chose France as a cradle of modern culture and civilization.

The French language, before entering Persia, was already the language of culture of eastern countries such as the Ottoman Empire whose cultural influence was very interesting for Persian scholars who read Turkish books. Thus, French poetry and literature, once they spread in Persia, influenced theatrical texts, especially comedy.

For centuries, comedy was basically based on Persian spectacular forms, such as Taghlid, a type of comedy criticizing the government. People liked this form and obviously European comedy, for its content, and it was appreciated by the Persians.

Tragedy, by contrast, especially the famous European tragedies which resembled the Ta'ziyah, could not enjoy success in Persia due to the lack of a popular language and the difficulty in adapting them with respect to Persian popular culture.

However, at an early stage, this literary output arrived in the country in two languages other than Persian: Turkish and French. Turkish was the language of the Ottoman Empire, with which Persia had many relations, due to its geographical proximity. French, on the other hand, was the language of the most important theatrical culture of the time, which is why many Persian students went first to France. Within a short time, French became the first foreign language spoken at court.

Another reason for the growing fascination that France exerted on Persian students is that it represents the highest and most elegant theatrical expression in the world. The French theatre has therefore symbolized a beacon for the theatrical cultures of many countries around the world.[285]

The highest point of French culture (theatrical or otherwise) is undoubtedly represented by the figure of Molière, pseudonym of Jean-Baptiste Poquelin. Every Persian student who visited the European courts came into contact with the cultural imprint left by the French, which sanctioned a real turning point in world theatrical and literary culture. The diffusion of Molière was also facilitated by the great linguistic force of his works. The writer, unlike others, was better able to adapt to what was the Persian cultural reality. When, by contrast, Persian students went to Russia or England they were unable to fully absorb the cultural and theatrical characteristics of these countries as they were far from Persian culture.[286]

Knowledge of the French language at court facilitated the knowledge of other authors such as Victor Hugo, Alexandre

---

[285] Jamshid Malek pur, *Persian dramatic literature*, [Adabīyāt-i namāyishī dar Īrān], (Tehran, Tus, 1983), 305.
[286] Ibid, 305-306.

Dumas and Voltaire. A further diffusion of French is due to the various teachings held in the Dar ol-Fonoun school, where this language was taught to many students, so that, when they went around the European courts, they could use it as a language of communication.

The teaching of French at the Dar al-Fonoun school was also facilitated by the construction of a theatre near the university itself: the students who studied French were thus able to translate and learn the French texts then recited in that theatre. Usually the translators who wanted to translate a script from another language tried to adapt it to Persian society, and the main aim was to broaden the cultural vision of Persia, a country still backward in terms of not only literary and artistic but also scientific knowledge, outside its national borders.

We have said that tragedy with respect to comedy had little diffusion in Persian society and practically Persian translators and writers later met the famous European tragic authors. A writer whose texts later arrived in Persian society is Pierre Corneille, who, along with Molière and Racine, was one of the three great French playwrights of the seventeenth century. He wrote thirty-five plays of various genres such as tragedies and comedies, but he was known to Persian society later than Molière.

Corneille's texts were in a language with a structure unknown to the Persians of the Qajar period, and translators had difficulty making his texts understood. However, the knowledge of Corneille at the beginning was only linked to his name and to some passages of his texts which, during the reign of Naser al Din Shah, were translated by various writers and translators such as Etemad ol Saltaneh and Mohammad Taher Mirza Eskandari: for example, the great Etemad ol Saltaneh in the second volume of his history of Naseri cites him as one of the greatest French writers. Or again, the same

Etemad ol Saltaneh in the manuscript, recounts a productive branch in the works of Voltaire:

> Voltaire was great because there was a poor girl in France who was Pierre Corneille's granddaughter. He helped and educated her and then contributed money to prepare her for her life, made her marry a noble boy and at her wedding he said: «I was like a soldier towards the family of her captain. This means that compared to Pierre Corneille you feel like a student before the master.[287]

The second person who during the reign of Naser al Din Shah spoke of Corneille was Prince Mohamad Taher Mirza Eskandari,[288] translator among other things of Alexandre Dumas's[289] volume *Louis XIV et son siècle.*

Pierre Corneille's lack of presence in Persian society during the reign of Naser al Din Shah made him one of the cultural objects of Persian translators. This shortcoming was also felt in the reign of Mozafar al-Din Shah and in the period of the Persian Constitutional Revolution, marked by internal wars, at the end of the reign of Mohamad Ali Shah.

It is in this period that many travelers went to Europe: among these there were intellectuals, who when they returned to Persia brought back much news regarding the theatre.

A totally different reason that instead pushed some of the strongly nationalist translators was the denunciation of the

---

[287] A manuscript by Etemad ol saltaneh, a productive branch in the works of Voltaire, Tehran, 1887, is found at central library of Tehran University.

[288] He was the son of Abbas Mirza and grandson of Fat'h Ali Shah Qajar. He was governor of Khoy and Salmas in 1832-1834 and governor of Qazvin 1848-1852. He died at the age of 46, 1856 in Tabriz. He is the ancestor of the Eskandari-Qajar family.

[289] Alexandre Dumas, translator Mohamad Taher Mirza Eskandari, *Louis XIV et son siècle*,(Tehran, Danesh mozafari, 1904).

problems of European society, showing the people how much Persian society, apparently backward in European eyes, actually had more positive aspects and values.

It was only later that other languages such as English and German also arrived in Persia, English with Shakespeare's texts and German with those of Schiller.

Last but not least, in Armenian society the use of languages such as English and German was known and widespread, from which the theatrical texts in the Armenian language, often represented in Persian, were translated. This fact demonstrates the need for a Persian translation of those texts.

The link between the Persian culture of the Qajar era and the dramaturgy of Molière was also important. His works spread in Persia through various routes:[290]

• Through direct translation from French into Persian within the country;

• Through information about his life published in the press or in books;

• Through Persian travelers, students and politicians who for various reasons went abroad;

• Through European travelers and politicians who went to Persia;

• Through Armenian theatre companies in Persia;

• Through the Dar al Fonun theatre which presented some European shows and above all the comedies of Molière.

Another factor that contributed to the diffusion of French and Molière was undoubtedly sanctioned by the political

---

[290] Niyayesh Pur hassan, *Iranians' recognition movement with Moliere*, (Tehran, Kuleh Poshti, 2019), 143.

affinities between Paris and Tehran. For example, a common factor of this period is characterized by the affirmation of the bourgeoisie which, albeit in different cultural contexts, takes hold in both countries.

Despite the great similarities, Persian and French societies had profound cultural and social divergences. While in France, for example, the first workers' revolts and their respective strikes began to occur, in Persia society was still anchored to a medieval conception, with landed properties and servants who worked without any privileges.

Molière's works have enjoyed a vast affirmation also for two important reasons: firstly, because their characters are not individuals of aristocratic classes, but belong to the lower middle class; this was a component that was of particular interest in Persia, as it reflected a large part of the population. The second reason is due to the fact that the struggle between the forces of good and evil was always present in the works of the French author; this feature was considered very important by Persian culture which favored works of that genre over works that dealt with other issues (such as those found in Shakespeare's works).[291]

In Molière's works, it is possible to find protagonists who joke and have many relationships with members of the court and individuals of high status and language. The same happens, for example, in the Takhte Hozi play, where we have the Siah joking with kings, princes, and other aristocratic characters.

Another important work by the French is *Le Misanthrope*, written in 1666, but translated into Persian only in 1864. For the first time, it was interpreted by the actor Mirza Habib Isfahani (1829 -1893). The first translation of *Le Misanthrope* was adapted in a way that was not faithful to the original, but

---

[291] Jamshid Malek pur, *Persian dramatic literature*, [Adabīyāt-i namāyishī dar Īrān], 316.

still able to say what was conveyed in that dramaturgy. It must be said that, after this text, various artists translated other works, such as *Tartuffe* and *Don Giovanni.*

In that same period, a class of intellectuals developed in Persia who, having traveled to the European courts and having lived in contact with new realities, attempted to open new horizons of thought in Persia. Mirza Habib Isfahani, in particular, is considered by scholars to be the father of the current Persian language. The cause of this recognition also lies in the translation work, carried out by the author, on three important works: *Haji Baba Isfahani*, *Gil Blas* and *Le Misanthrope*, of which mention has already been made. His great passion for travel meant that Mirza knew several languages, such as Turkish, Arabic and French.[292]

Another important Persian character is Mirza Jafar Gharache Daghi, who belongs to the category of intellectuals mentioned above, and who was the first to illustrate the reality of the dramatic genre to Persian culture. He too knew the Turkish and French languages and tried his hand at translating several works by Molière. Another work of translation authored by him consists of the works of Akhondzadeh.[293]

Yet another exponent of the intellectuals is the Azerbaijani writer Mirza Fatali Achundovo Akhondzadeh He was influenced by eighteenth-century French thought and Russian literature, and distinguished himself. He was as well the author of six plays, which make him the founder of the

---

[292] Jamshid Malek pur, *Persian dramatic literature*, [Adabīyāt-i namāyishī dar Īrān], 319-321.

[293] Akhondzadeh (1812 –1878), Azerbaijani and Persian writer, can be considered the main playwright of the Persian constitutional revolution period.

Azerbaijani theatre, to say nothing of his philosophical essays.[294]

Prince Haji Mohammad Taher Mirza (Tabriz, 1821 – Tehran, 1896) is credited with several translations of works by Dumas, such as *The Count of Monte Cristo* and *The Three Musketeers*. He also wrote some works such as *The Marriage of Mr. Taher Mirza* which are undoubtedly influenced by a play such as Molière's *Forced Marriage*. As has already been said, on the other hand, the strong link between the court of Tehran and Paris is due to various factors, not only political, but also commercial and cultural.
One notable influence is the significant impact of French theater on Persian theater.

7. People of theatre

As we have already explained, the Qajar era is a special period for Persian entertainment, full of theatrical imports from European countries, and during which the experiences assimilated by Persian scholars and travelers in Europe are poured into the homeland, influencing Persian culture and theatrical literature. There was a special interest on the part of Persians of noble or high cultural rank in learning foreign languages (primarily French) and European literary and theatrical art forms. Among them we present some personalities who have had a great influence on literature and theatrical culture.

Etemad ol Saltaneh (1843-1896)

Surely one of the most important people who influenced Qajar society was Mohamad Hasan Khan Etemad ol

---

[294] Jamshid Malek pur, *Persian dramatic literature*, [Adabīyāt-i namāyishī dar Īrān], 122-137.

Saltaneh. Etemad ol Saltaneh (a man in whom the king puts his trust) was the title that the king offered to one who was a Persian politician, translator and journalist. His family worked for the Qajar government for years. He studied at Dar ol Fonun School, where he learned French, and went to Paris to continue studying.

Much information comes from his diary, in which for years he noted daily what was happening in the city and, above all, the relationship he had with the king. Only his wife was aware of this, who was the one who sometimes wrote down what her husband said. He had been in Paris for four years and had picked up many cultural and, in particular, theatrical influences. As soon as he returned to Persia he became the king's personal translator. He worked in various political positions and eventually became minister of culture.

From his works it can be understood that Mohamad Hasan Khan knew history and art very well, for having lived for years in Europe he could easily translate famous French books. He was one of the people close to the king and spent a lot of time in his company. In fact, in his diary he says that the king wanted to hear the newspapers and books and Etemad ol Saltane read them for him. The king liked world history and the memoirs of European travelers. He also usually accompanied King Naser al Din Shah on all the trips he made. For twenty-five years he had always followed the king, even on trips to Europe. But the king did not have much faith in him; indeed, some scholars believe that he was in charge of the spies of the Qajar court. The causes of his death are unknown.[295]

Though educated in France, Mohamad Hasan Khan had decided to work with the Russian government in Persia, and the king apparently did not trust him. But still with all the

---

[295] Jamshid Malek pur, *Persian dramatic literature*, [Adabīyāt-i namāyishī dar Īrān], 339.

work he did both translating and writing about him, he had a great influence on Persian theatre. As culture minister he often invited ambassadors from foreign countries to watch Persian theatre performances and their workings. Another important aspect of his life that we can underline are two works, of which we have indirect sources today: these speak of the Persian theatre, above all of the changes that take place in the theatre after the king's travels in Europe. The first is the newspaper *Iran*, the second is his travel memoirs, called *Journal of Etemad ol Saltaneh.*[296]

Mozaian al- Doleh (1847-1894)

Mirza Ali Akbar Khan naghash Bashi, called Mozaian al-Dole, was born in Kashan in 1847. He was one of the first who, by order of the Shah of Persia Naser al-din Shah, went to France to continue his education. He studied the performing arts and, upon returning to Persia, began teaching at the school of Dar ol Fonun. He translated some theatrical texts, especially by Molière, and on behalf of the king of Persia himself he started teaching European theatre, setting up for the first time *Le Misanthrope* by Molière. With his knowledge of European theatre and Persian theatre he attempted to devise a new form of comedy that would integrate both, as audiences would not immediately accept the form imported from Europe.[297]

---

296 According to my research, I came to the conclusion that one of the most mysterious characters of the Qajar period is Mohamad Hasan Khan Etemad ol Saltaneh. He was one of the closest people to the king, and he had a lot of confidential information about the king and his decisions. It was proved to me personally that he narrated many historical events in the Shah's travels in a different way or did not write at all. Especially in the face of dramatic events that took place during the Shah's travels, this is quite tangible. Perhaps he can be mentioned as the biggest censor of the theatre in the Qajar period.

297 Mostafa Oskuee, *History of Iranian Theater*, [Pizhūhishī dar tārīkh-i ti'ātr-i Īran], 159.

Zahir ol Dole (1864-1924).

Ali Khan Zahir ol Dole was an important politician of the Qajar dynasty. Born in Tehran, he founded the Okhovat institute, built in 1886. What developed here was a sort of fraternity between different characters who declared themselves neither politicians nor important members of society, but whose membership in Freemasonry was subsequently proven. Such was the main component that would characterize this institution.[298]

Zahir ol Dole loved theater, both Persian and European. His home was a popular place to perform plays and shows. Sometimes he worked as a theatre producer and was professional in pantomime staging.

Zahir ol Dole accompanied Mozafar al Din Shah on his first trip to Europe and also accompanied the king to all the shows he attended, as he did on the monarch's subsequent visits to Europe. We can interpret his desire to see European plays as a way of being influenced and in turn influencing Persian theatre culture, in a constant process of updating and renewing Persian society through the performing arts.

Naser ol Molk (1856 –1927).

Abol Ghasem Khan Naser ol Molk was a politician and ruler of the time of Naser al Din Shah. He was one of the princes who often accompanied the king of Persia on his travels in Europe. Fine connoisseur of the main European languages, he translated for the king works such as Shakespeare's *The Merchant of Venice* and *Othello.*[299]

---

298 Yaghub Azhand, *Theatre of the Qajars*,(Namāyish dar dawrah-i Qājār), 557.

299 Mehdi Malekzade, *History of the Iranian Constitutional Revolution*, [Tārīkh-i inqilāb-i mashrụṭīyat-i Īrān], (Tehran, Sokhan 2004), 550.

Moaied ol Mamalek (1869-1916).

Morteza Gholi Khan, called Moaied ol Mamalek, was a Persian author and journalist who studied in Dar ol Fonun and then went to Baku to practice. He was a translator of European works, of which *Cyrus the Great* and *Old Governors, the New Governors* are remembered. As soon as he returned from Baku he started a newspaper called the *Persian Police*. No doubt he was one of the most influential authors of Persian theatrical literature. In his works one can see the disorder of the society of the Qajar period, especially at the time of the Persian Constitutional Revolution.

He had to travel extensively abroad, especially to Egypt and Turkey, to escape repression at home due to the subjects of his theatrical products, of which he was often both author and performer.[300]

Mirza Reza Naini (1873- ?).

Mirza Reza Khan Naini, called Ghazi Noor, was born in Brujerd. Persian author, journalist and politician, he knew Arabic and French. He was one of the followers of the Persian Constitutional Revolution and had close relations with the commanders of the Revolution.

Mirza Reza was the first to found in Persia a magazine specifically dedicated to the theatre, in fact the journalists of his newspaper, entitled *Theatre*, went to criticize performances, both Persian and from other countries, and published reviews and some theatrical texts translated into Persian.

Politically he was aligned in favor of the humblest, and in fact during the reign of Ahmad Shah, when the people needed

---

[300] Abolghasem Janati Ataee, *Iranian Theatre*, [Bunyād-i namāyish dar Īrān], (Tehran ,Safi Al Shah, 1977), 116-117.

grain and Ahmad Shah did not give permission to open the doors of the warehouses to help the needy, Mirza Reza Naini denounced him and brought him in front of the court. He thought that with the theatre, people could approach culture and abandon ignorance.[301]

Kamal ol Vezare (1874- ?).

Ahmad Mahmudi called Kamal ol Vezare was a Persian politician and author born in Tehran. Like the other intellectuals, he went to the school of Dar ol fonun, where he studied Arabic and French, Persian literature and mathematics. He worked at the Persian embassy as a secretary. He was one of the followers of the Persian Constitutional Revolution and joined the secret group known as "The Society of Punishment," in revolt against people who in their view opposed national interests.

In his works there is a structured dramaturgy with strong influences from the European theatre. The most important masterpiece of his is *Ostad noruz pine duz*.[302]

Mirza Agha Tabrizi (? -1915)

Mirza Agha Tabrizi was the one who first ventured into writing scripts in the Persian language. During the Qajar period, he made significant contributions to Persian theatrical literature. He studied at the Dar ol Fonun School and, given his knowledge of foreign languages, he began working in the Baghdad embassy in Istanbul, to return to Tehran after years to work in the French embassy.

---

[301] Yaghub Azhand, *Theatre of the Qajars*,(Namāyish dar dawrah-i Qājār), 560-564.
[302] Ibid 556.

He wrote Five plays, the manuscripts of which we still have today, and translated numerous articles and other plays from different languages. He is one of the first people who created Persian drama by integrating it with European drama style. Among his most important works, we can mention: *The Story of Ashraf Khan*, *The Way of Governing Zemam Khan*, *The Story of Haji Morshed the Magician*, and *The Love Story of Hashem Khan*, and *The Story of Karbala's Journey by Haj Gholi Mirza.*[303]

Gregory Yeghikian (1880-1951)

Gregory Yeghikian was an Armenian author, journalist and translator who spoke Turkish, Persian and English. He studied in Venice and also spoke Italian. Unable to bear the violence of the Ottomans, in 1896 he emigrated from Armenia to Persia, where he tried to found a political group of Armenians, but had to face multiple problems.

Subsequently, he decided to translate and write texts that had freedom and democracy[304] as their theme. For a time he was a translator for an Iranian revolutionary hero, Mirza Kuchik Khan.

His works can be divided into two groups: historical and moral. He too, with the translations made both in Persian and in Armenian, had great influence on Persian theatrical literature.[305]

Ali Nasr (1891–1961)

---

[303] Jamshid Malek pur, *Persian dramatic literature*, [Adabīyāt-i namāyishī dar Īrān], 195.

[304] (1880 - 1921) Active during the Qajar period he was one of the commanders of the Persian constitutional revolution in the north of the country.

[305] Yaghub Azhand, *Theatre of the Qajars*,(Namāyish dar dawrah-i Qājār), 575.

Undoubtedly, one of the greatest cultural and theatrical figures of Iran, who had a very constructive role in the theater in later generations, was Sayed Ali Nasr. Founder of the Iran comedy and the first acting academy[306] in Iran, he tried to promote the art of theatre in a completely scientific and methodical way in Iran with the cultural assets of Iran and what he learned from the European theatre. His scientific and practical activities in Iranian theatre encouraged many adults who were trained in the acting academy to enter the professional field of theatre. Owing to his unique efforts and activities, he is known as the father of Iranian theatre.

Ali Nasr, in addition to having a complete knowledge of Iranian culture and society, was well acquainted with European theatrical culture, especially that of France and Italy, and this was the reason why he was able to transfer part of the modern knowledge of European theatre to Iran. But all of his art did not end here, for he was someone who could integrate both European and Iranian theatrical forms with full knowledge and stage shows that were attractive to popular and intellectual audiences as well as having a correct and up-to-date framework and structure. This was something that could only be done by Sayed Ali Nasr.

At any rate, Ali Nasr, knowing other Iranians who tried to translate and import European theatre to Iran before him, tried hard to do so and made many efforts. The result of the efforts of raising a generation with knowledge of Iranian theatre was that each of them somehow influenced the new season of Iranian theatre.

Zabih Behruz (1890-1971)

Zabih Behrouz was an Iranian historian, author, playwright and linguist. He was born in Tehran, where he studied at the

[306] It was founded in ۱۹۳۸ in Tehran and on Laleh zar Street.

American school, and then in Egypt and England. During his stay in England, he worked for Professor Edward Granville Browne, orientalist and researcher at Cambridge. Behrouz returned to his homeland in 1923 and began writing some works such as *Jijak Ali Shah*, in which, for example, the main target was the tyrannical monarchy of Naser al-Din Shah Qajar.

His lyrics are characterized by a vintage style. As we have mentioned, his most famous theatrical play was *Jijak Ali Shah*, but he also wrote other plays on historical subjects: *The King of Persia*, *The Lady of Armenia*, *In the Road of Love*, and *The Night of Ferdowsi.* [307]

Hasan Moghadam (1898-1925).

He was an author, journalist and one of the most important intellectuals in the last years of the Qajar government. He spoke French and English. He studied in Switzerland for eleven years and knew famous European writers and authors. After completing his studies in Switzerland, he went to Istanbul and worked in the Persian embassy. After that he went to work in Egypt where he died of disease.

Having studied in Europe he was familiar with the European form and techniques of writing. He collaborated with a newspaper called *Etehad* (Unity), where he wrote about European politics and economics.

A theatre lover, he wrote various theatrical texts, among which the most important is *Jafar Khan az farangh barghashte* (Jafar Khan has Returned from Abroad), which from a structural point of view takes on a form similar to the European one. His writings composed outside Persian territory have been published under the name of Pierrot

[307] Yaghub Azhand, *Theatre of the Qajars*,(Namāyish dar dawrah-i Qājār), 566-567.

Malade. One of his important works of research is a collection of Persian newspapers from the period of the First World War.[308]

Reza Kamal Shahrzad (1898 –1937)

Reza kamal Shahrzad was a Persian author, director, translator active in the last years of the Qajar government. He knew traditional Persian music and played the tar, in addition to speaking French, English, and Turkish. One of his important translations from French was that of Oscar Wilde's *Salome.* Usually his plays were staged at the Grand Hotel in Tehran. Another important translation of his was Victor Hugo's *Hernani.*[309]

Another important Persian character is Mirza Jafar Ghara Che Daghi.[310] Who belongs to the category of intellectuals mentioned above, and who was the first to illustrate the reality of the dramatic genre to Persian culture. He too knew the Turkish and French languages and tried his hand at translating several works by Molière. Another translation work written by him consists of the works of Mirza Fatali Akhundov. [311].

Another exponent of the intellectuals is the Azerbaijani writer Mirza Fatali Achundovo (Akhond zadeh) He was influenced by eighteenth-century French thought and Russian literature, and distinguished himself, as well as the author of six plays,

---

308 Yaghub Azhand, *Theatre of the Qajars*,(Namāyish dar dawrah-i Qājār), 570-571.

309 Ibid 572.

310 Persian translator and author (1834-1892) knew various languages such as Turkish. Was translated various texts by other Persian writer Mirza Fatali Akhundov

311 Akhondzadeh (1812 –1878), Azerbaijani and Persian writer, can be considered the main playwright of the Persian constitutional revolution period.

which make him the founder of the Azerbaijani theater, even for some philosophical essays.

Opera and musical comedy

Another European form that strongly influenced Persian theatre is musical theatre, particularly in the genres of opera and musical comedy. In the history of Persian theatre of previous centuries, it was a tradition for actors to use music in their performances, especially of the traditional genre. The musical intervention was usually in the opening and closing moments, and this practice has been perpetuated for centuries, according to the taste of the public. This tradition prevailed until the Qajar period, in which new theatrical productions appeared to be an integration between ancient forms and the genres of recent European import that were gradually taking hold in Persia, giving life to new artistic experiences and new forms of entertainment. However, musical performances are also found in the ancient period before the affirmation of Islam when the actors, acting, sang, and played a genre called Gusan. There was also another type of spectacular play called Ghavali where the actors sang and played and usually told a short story.[312] Subsequently, when the Islamic religion spread in Persia, these actors could not continue acting as in the past and this spectacular form lost its importance. From this form they moved on to another important form called Naghali, which used body movements, using a wooden stick called Metragh.

For the Persians musical performances were not unheard of, but in Qajar society musical performances were not performed for religious reasons.

---

[312] Mary Boyce, translator Mehri Sharafi, *The Parthian Gosans in Iran*, (Tehran Chista, 1990), 756-780.

Persian travelers who had the opportunity to attend these performances then brought the information back to their homeland, marking the beginning of an increasingly frequent collaboration between European and Persian singers and actors. The interest in these types of performances shown by the Qajar dynasty is significant, thanks mainly to the European trips of Naser al Din Shah and Mozafar al Din Shah made to countries where these forms were particularly felt. On these trips the royal family was often accompanied by theatre artists who in turn brought their impressions back to the Persian theatre.

The introduction of European spectacularity would not have been understood without a gradual passage of styles progressively grafted onto the traditional spectacular form.

The musical instruments usually used in Persian performances were traditional or of oriental origin, and the singing was the traditional Persian one. A peculiarity was constituted by the role of the actresses: until the Qajar period women could not be on stage and usually the young males acted *en travesti*. It was crucial at that point for Persian artists to find a solution to this cultural gap. Usually the companies that came from abroad had their own actresses, but when a Persian group wanted to make an opera or a musical comedy they sometimes used Armenian or other actresses from other countries that could represent these spectacular forms. The profession of actress for Persian women was still not foreseen.

The use of music was an important reason for paving the way for opera in Persia. Just at that time, at the Grand Hotel in Tehran, it was customary to perform various operas, and in particular Bizet's *Carmen*, albeit in Russian. The famous singer Aghabaief, who performed in the same opera, was able to thrill the audience with her singing. Subsequently another famous singer, also Armenian, called Mrs. Abuiana represented the operetta *Arshin Mal Alan*[313] by composer Uzeyir Hajibeyov in the Azerbaijani language. During the same period she had performed another play called *Adam and Eve.*

To import art and above all entertainment, the city of Tabriz was important due to its geographical position: Russian and Azeri actors could enter Persia through the city. Therefore, the first influences of a different art start right from Tabriz, in the Azeri language, which was very easy to understand for the inhabitants of Tabriz. Gradually these works spread to the capital and to other cities of Persia, initiating innovations in spectacular forms, in the use of language and music, and also in other theatrical genres.

Among the various Persian and foreign artists who represented these spectacular forms in the Qajar period, there was Uzeyir Hajibeyov, a great Azerbaijani musician and writer (1885-1948), the first opera composer in Islamic countries. At the end of his studies he was in Moscow to continue studying music. After two years he wanted to move to St. Petersburg but it was not financially possible for him. Thanks to the knowledge he had of Persian performances, he tried to integrate these two spectacular forms, writing famous works on folk themes characteristic of Azerbaijan. In 1937 Hajibeyo wrote his most famous work, entitled *Kor oglu.*[314] With the help of leaders of the Persian Constitutional Revolution, such as Nariman Narimanof,[315] and Jalil Mohamad Gholizade, he would later have great influence on the progress of Persian musical comedy. Uzeyir Hajibeyov's value lay in mixing Azerbaijani music with classical form, as

---

313 A popular romantic comic opera of Azerbaijan from 1913.

314 Means: son of a blind man. It was a Persian, Azeri mythological Opera in 5 acts.

315 An Azerbaijani political writer journalist (1870 –1925)

we can first observe in the opera *Leyli and Majnun.*[316]

In the early years when musical operas and comedies were being performed in Persia, most of the indigenous scholars and religious people did not want to accept these spectacular forms, preferring traditional Persian music without any modification.

In the period of the Constitutional Revolution[317] there were various groups that performed the work in various cities of Persia, while other Persian composers began to write new works: important among these was *Kave*, recited by more than sixty foreign actors.

In 1922, during one of the last years of the Qajar period, Ali Naghi Vaziri[318] with the cooperation of Said Nafisi,[319] Kamal Shahrzad[320] and others founded a music club. This club where Persian and foreign actors and Armenian actresses performed, quickly became very famous and was a meeting point for Persian intellectuals and left-wing politicians. But unfortunately after two years a fire decreed the end of the musical club.[321]

---

[316] It is the first Azerbaijani national opera written by Uzeyir Hajibeyov in 1907; the story is taken from the famous Persian poet Nizami Ganjavi (1141 - 1209).

[317] The Persian Constitutional Revolution was a movement against the reign of the last Qajar Shahs. The constitution was signed by Mozafar al din Shah on August 6, 1906.

[318] (1887 -1979) Persian musician and composer .He put many influences on traditional Persian music.

[319] (1895 - 1966) historian, writer, Persian translator was one of the first professor of the University of Tehran

[320] (1898 –1937) Persian poet and theater writer. He was the first person that women were protagonists in his works.

[321] Yaghub Azhand, *Theatre of the Qajars*,(Namāyish dar dawrah-i Qājār), 468.

CHAPTER 4:

PERSIAN COMEDY'S AFFINITY WITH THE COMMEDIA DELL'ARTE

The first and most important point in analyzing and comparing Iranian and Italian history, art and culture is the abundance of similarities between the two countries in these fields. In certain periods, both countries have influenced each other, especially in the field of culture and art.

Commedia dell'Arte originated in the early sixteenth century in its native Italy. This innovative and universal theatrical art, in an arc-shaped journey, was first published in France and then in Spain, and after returning to Italy, it was established as a stable theatrical form and reached many parts of the world, including Persia, and its enormous impact has been shown around the world.

At the time, Iran was under the rule of the Safavid government, and there the arts primarily focused on religious themes. Iranian comedy, which has its roots in Iran's past, has undergone some changes during this time. However, the basic shape of the Persian Comedy (Takht-e Hozi) was created during this period. The similarities between these two forms of comedy are revealed by examining them. This chapter will discuss the similarities and potential mutual effects of these two types of theatre.

Historical look

With a quick look at the relations between Iran and Italy, one can understand the close ties between these two ancient cultures and civilizations. From ancient times until now, there have been close exchanges and connections between different cultures, including the rich biculturalism of

Mithraism. One notable example is the spread of Mithraism rituals to ancient Rome. The great Greek historian Plutarch says, "The Romans became acquainted with Mithraism through Sicilian sailors who had traveled from a state in Asia Minor."[322]

Along with the Mithraism ritual, commercial communication was considered one of the most significant interactions between these two cultures. This interaction occurred from ancient Rome to the Qajar period and continued under various titles.

Another significant aspect to contemplate is the notable scientific and cultural link between Persia and the Romans, exemplified by Jundishapur University. This esteemed institution thrived due to the presence of esteemed professors from Rome and Greece, as well as ancient Indian physicians.

After the fall of the Roman and Persian empires, the relations between the two cultures became strained for a while. The first time peace and stability were established between these two countries was during the Ilkhanate period, facilitated by Italian merchants. A merchant named Buscarello, who hailed from the renowned Ghisulfi family in the port of Genoa, can be considered as one of the first to regularly engage with fellow merchants. The latter came to Iran for business.[323]

During the period of Shah Abbas, which is known as the friendliest period of relations between Iran and Italy, many travelers, including Pietro Della Valle,[324] came to Iran. These commercial relations continued until then. Today, there are

---

[322] Martin Vermazern, *Mithraism*, translated by Bozorg Naderzad, (Tehran, Cheshmeh, 2001), 31.

[323] Mria Francesca Tiepolo, *La ripubblica di Venezia*, transleated by Iraj Anvar, (Tehran 1973), 5.

[324] Pietro della valle (Roma 1586 – Roma, 1652).

travelogues of most of these travelers, which are sometimes used as important presentation documents.

In the field of dramaturgy, during the mid-sixteenth century, Italy saw the development of the Commedia dell'Arte, while in Persia, a form of theatrical performance similar to comedy called Taghlid emerged. However, the diffusion of these two theatrical genres takes place in different ways. While the Italian phenomenon expands towards the great European capitals, on a continental scale, the Taghlid develops only on a regional level within Persia itself, without crossing national borders.

Persian theatre, in its new version, is a contemporary adaptation of traditional Iranian works that emerged during the Safavid period, coinciding with the resumption of Iran's relations with the West. In the meantime, the trips of Westerners to Iran and Iranians to the West had a significant impact on Iran's theatre.

Among Persian travelers in the Safavid period, especially to Venice, we must remember Haj Mohammad,[325] "Musa Beyk,"[326] "Naghd Ali Beyk,"[327] Mohammad Zaman,[328] "Oruj Beyk,"[329] and Mohammad "Reza Beyk," the last one a Persian ambassador during the reign of Shah Sultan Hoseyn. Indeed, during the course of his travels, he had seen European shows. He visited the court of Louis XIV, where he attempted to strengthen the relationship between Persia and France. "Mohammad Reza Beyk," the first person to visit European theatre buildings during his trip to Paris, tried to

325 Persian ambassador during the reign of Uzun Hasan, in Venice in 1471.

326 Ambassador of Shah Abbas I. In 1625 he went to Holland.

327 Ambassador of Shah Abbas I. In 1626 he went to England.

328 He was a famous painter of the Safavid period. In 1650 he went to Venice and other Italian cities.

329 He was one of the Persian ambassadors from the time of Abbas I who traveled to Europe in search of alliances against the Ottoman Empire. They called him Don Giovanni Persian.

learn about European lifestyles. Therefore, he would occasionally attend performances. Herbert Morris, in his book entitled *Mohammad Reza Beyk, Persian Minister in the Court of Louis XIV*, provides a report in which he states: "On December 15th, 1714, they invited Mohammad Reza Beyk to see the opera."[330] The stage where he was supposed to be was designed in the Eastern style. Two individuals who were fluent in French translated it. Mohammad Reza Beyk had ordered that some gifts, such as leather dresses, be presented to two dancers. He sent coffee and tea to the director of the project. After two days, they still had not invited him to continue working, and he was disappointed that his efforts had gone unnoticed. As soon as Mohammad Reza Beyk noticed that the gifts were somewhat worn, he still appreciated them and generously gave the girls gold coins along with valuable Persian fabrics. On December 20, the Commander of the Navy of Marseille invited him, along with other commanders, to a farewell dinner for "Mohammad Reza Beyk" before his departure to oversee the final work. But, as it was mentioned, Iran's relations with Italy grew during the Safavid era as a result of political, commercial, and religious factors. Meanwhile, many travelers came to Iran. An important aspect that serves as valuable evidence of the show today is the existence of travelogues written by these travelers. These travelogues provide detailed accounts of various types of Persian performances.

With the arrival of the Qajars and Naser al-Din Shah, Iran entered a new era. Relations between Iran and Western countries have improved, and as a result, there has been an increase in visits by Western artists to Iran and in Iranians traveling to the West. Naser al-Din Shah, who held a deep fascination for art, dreamed of traveling to Europe. This dream became the driving force behind his multiple trips to

---

330 Herbert Morris, *Mohammad Reza Beyk Persian Ambassador in the court of Louis XIV*, Abdol Hoseyn Vojdani, ,(Tehran, Gozaresh 1 983), 61-63.

the continent. Naser al-Din Shah's reign can be mentioned as one of the most influential periods in Iranian theatre.

Naser al-Din Shah's trips to Europe can be considered a pivotal moment for the process of Europeanization. Maybe when the Shah was watching theatre at the Royal Albert Hall and other theatres in Europe, he wanted to have plays in the same style at "Dowlat's Theatre" and other Iranian theatres.

In the first years after its opening, Dowlat's theatre was used solely for religious performances (Tazie) and for some official meetings between governing officials. Later, it also hosted stage plays. At any rate, and as mentioned earlier, the reign of Naser al-Din Shah marked the beginning of a period of significant changes in Iran. And, of course, these changes happened in culture and art, especially in theatre. One of the significant events that occurred during the Qajar period was the establishment of the Persian comedy (Takhte Hozi), which closely resembled its Italian counterpart. It is worth noting that its origins can be traced back to the sixteenth century.

Now, with the aforementioned introduction, we will discuss the similarities and differences between both forms of theatre.

In a land where happy moments in life are scarce, the few comic plays that exist are often bitter and filled with criticism. Criticism that can only be brought to the stage through a play and by comedians, rather than with a real face, but behind a mask or makeup, is something that statesmen and politicians cannot restrict or eliminate. In the middle of the Safavid era, there were comedians and musicians who attended the parties of nobles in major cities. They would perform dances, songs, and entertaining plays. From the development and evolution of these intermezzos in the Western world, a type of play called Mazhakeh[331] emerged. Mazhakeh included short stories accompanied by musical instruments, singing, running, chasing, and comic beatings performed by several actors.

From the continuation and progress of the Mazhakeh, the Taglid play was born. In this play, the songs were reduced and the story line became much fuller. In this type of play, the actors attempted to imitate various dialects from different cities of Iran. One of the most significant aspects of this play was the actors' improvisation, which was warmly received by the audience.

It can be said that towards the end of the Safavid period, imitation shows began to be held in coffee houses in certain large and bustling cities. Actors adapted their style to cater to the audience's preferences, leading to the creation of innovative methods to entertain people.

With the passage of time, changes were made to the story and the form of impersonation, making this show more attractive to people. One of the changes was in the dance routine, where four dancers wearing different colors (red, yellow, blue, and purple) were concealed inside four boxes. Several individuals then brought the boxes onto the stage. A little later, the music started playing, and the boxes were opened one by one. The dancers performed both individually and collectively before returning to their respective boxes. The idea of creating this type of show can be related to a marquee play. Over time, the purple dancer was replaced by an actor wearing blackface makeup. The show, titled *Four Chests*, is how it made its way into the imitation play.[332]

---

331 Mazhakeh literally means something or someone that causes a funny thing to happen.

332 Beyzaee Bahram, *Theatre in Iran*, [Namāyish dar Īrān], (Tehran, Kavian, 1965), 167-169

Another form of Persian play that emerged after the Taqlid was the Baghal bazi, which belongs to the genre of master and servant plays. In this play, there was a wealthy and miserly master or grocer who typically employed a lazy and forgetful servant. This servant often failed to comprehend his master's instructions and carried them out in a different manner, resulting in amusing and comical situations.

But it was during the Zand period that individual and itinerant actors joined together, giving rise to new imitation groups. With the expansion of urbanization, these shows were being performed more frequently. With the arrival of the Qajars and Tehran becoming the capital, such groups became more integrated into the city. During the Qajar period, a show called Takhte Hozi, which had its origins in the comic Safavid shows and possibly even earlier, was created.

Common Points between Takht Hozi and Commedia dell'arte

1. The Characters

There is no complete and written definition of Takht Hozei, but according to Davod Fath Ali Begi, one of the greatest Iranian theatre masters, Takht Hozei is a type of Iranian narrative play that combines comedy, folk elements, and semi-melodic elements. It is performed in the middle circle of the audience.

Fig. 65.Two character of Persian comedy (Siah) and commedia dell'arte(Pulcinella), Florance, Italy.

There are two main types, the Lord and the Black, in Takht Hozi, and most of the time the story is formed from their confrontation. Takht Hozi can be classified into four categories based on the subject matter: 1. Historical and mythological stories, such as those found in the *Shahnameh*. 2. Stories of Daily Life. 3. Imaginative plays such as *Four Sandogh*[333] and *Bald Champion* 4 are examples of pseudo-moral plays that are products of the new society.

In this type of comedy, the characters are completely clear. Now we will examine these types:

1-1. Haji Posh

He usually comes from the upper class of society. The title changes according to the subject of the character, but in

[333] Literally, it means four chests.

general, the characteristics of the characters remain fixed. Mostly, it is the opposite of the black character. If it is a historical story: he becomes either a king or a minister. If a dramatic event takes place in the present, he portrays the character of an elderly nobleman. These characters possess power and own palaces and properties. Most of them are stingy, greedy, insidious, and pretentious.

In the Commedia dell'Arte, the old men are called Magnifico, Pantalone, and others. They are always equipped with a mask and do not always speak in dialect. These characters are portrayed as rich and wise, but they are not always subjected to the grotesque satire that a simplistic tradition has assigned to them. They are often portrayed as hindering the marriages of young lovers, but they can do so even if they hold a high social rank. In such cases, their names are sometimes transformed to allude to sovereigns or oriental figures.[334]

2-1. Siah[335]

Undoubtedly, the most central role of this show is Siah, the servant. He carries the burden of comedy in the show. This character has a persuasive and discerning language. Sometimes his strength surpasses that of the hero in the story, while at other times his intelligence and knowledge rival those of scientists. Sometimes his laziness and lack of productivity define his personality. In general, the most important factor that makes this character stand out is the self-contradiction of his desires, which can be seen in that particular moment.

Among the other characters in this play, we can mention the young man or the lover, who is mostly supported by Siah.

---

[334] Siro Ferrone, *La Commedia dell'Arte. Italian actresses and actors in Europe (16th-18th centuries),* (Torino Einaudi, 2014), 85.

[335] Siah literally means black color, but it refers to the makeup of the actor in this role, which is black.

Another character that greatly contributes to the comedic aspect of the story is the womanizer. This character may either be forced to disguise themselves as a woman due to social and religious constraints, or they may be introduced as a comedic device based on the requirements of the plot.

The servant, dressed in red, symbolically evokes the renewal of the seasons. In the final five days of winter, multiple shows were held, one of which showcased Haji "Firuz." The protagonist, dressed in red, symbolizes the arrival of the New Year and the end of the cold winter season.

Ferrone believes that in the commedia dell'arte, the servant characters (Zanni) can generally be classified into two types. The first type is the clever and cunning "Zanni," who excels at creating and resolving complex intrigues. This character is driven by a desire for financial gain and is essentially a pragmatic manipulator of situations. The second type[336] is the clumsy and foolish "Zanni," also known as "Pasticcione" and "Balardo." This character is characterized by a nimble physique and insatiable appetites for both sex and food. This character resembles a mischievous lunatic rather than a conventional servant. Subsequently, other characters enter the scene wearing masks, such as the Vizier, the lovers, the old woman, and the religious figures, in accordance with the specific requirements of the staged comic episode. The common and, of course, very interesting point in both shows is the division of the characters into three groups: old men, servants, and lovers. In addition to these three groups, there are other characters that enter as needed for the story. Some other characters, such as Il Capitano in Commedia dell'arte, have counterparts like Darogh or Vizier Posh in Persian comedy.

---

[336] Siro Ferrone, *La Commedia dell'Arte. Italian actresses and actors in Europe (XVI-XVIII century).* 85-86.

In Persian comedy, masks are typically not used for characters, and usually they use makeup. Sometimes, a character wearing a mask can often be found in spectacles that have a fantasy or mythological theme. According to Cesare Molinari, the term "masks" was only used to describe the distinctive characters of the commedia dell'arte starting from the mid-seventeenth century.[337] The study hypothesizes that the mask was not the main focus of this theater: "The masks are important, but they are considered as one component among many, contributing to a delicate and uncertain balance that sometimes doesn't even include them." But the most important point in this case is the word "mask." In the Italian language, this word is called "Maschera," which refers to the mask as a display object and to the characters of Commedia dell'arte.

It is interesting that in Persian, the term "Maskhare" refers to a type or kind of comedian. Perhaps, the earliest uses of the word "Maskhare" can be traced back to a poem attributed to Obeid Zakani.[338]

رو مسخرگی پیشه کن و مطربی آموز

خواهی که شود بخت تو فرخنده و پیروز[339]

In addition, during the Safavid era, someone who was concerned about music and entertainment in the Safavid court was called a Maskhare Bashi.

---

[337] Cesare Molinari, *La Commedia dell'Arte*, (Milan, Mondadori, 1985), 15.
[338] Persian poet for 14 centuries
[339] Go and become Maskhareh (comedian) and learn to sing and playing music.

2. The "lazi" and the "Ghushe"

The term "lazzo" refers to a brief mimic and clownish action that is interspersed with dialogue to add liveliness to the scene. The lazzi is one of the most important techniques of the Commedia dell'Arte. Giacomo Oreglia, in his book entitled *La Commedia dell'Arte*,[340] discusses various jokes, including the joke of silencing. In this joke, while the master is speaking, Pulcinella interrupts him with his own words, and the master tries to get him to be quiet. This exchange happens three times, and in the end, when Punchinello speaks to his master, the master interrupts him and tells him to shut up. Or even the trick of the mosquitoes: when the owner asks Pulcinella who is at home, Pulcinella replies that there is not a single mosquito to be found. When the master enters the house and sees three of Pulcinella's friends and scolds him, Pulcinella replies, "You didn't find any mosquitoes, instead you found three people."

The Takhte Hozi show was created as a result of two implicit agreements—one between the actors and another between the actors and the spectators. The agreement between the actors and the spectators pertains to the progression of the scene itself. For instance, an actor may declare that upon hearing a specific word, all those in attendance must repeat it. Or, an actor uses a word, attributing to it a special and ambiguous meaning, which he illustrates to the audience but hides from the other characters in the play. In this way, a strong connection is created between the actor and the spectators.[341]

Another agreement concerns only the actors of the Takhte Hozi, who know how to regulate the progress of the performance based on a strong camaraderie that allows them

340 Giacomo, Oreglia, *La Commedia dell'Arte,* translator Natalie Choobineh, (Tehran Ghatreh, 2002), 39.

341 Yaghub Azhand, *Theatre of the Qajars*,[Namāyish dar dawrah-i Qājār], 286-287.

to alternate the various jokes that make up the show, called Ghushe, presented on stage simply by mentioning their titles. In the Takhte Hozi, there is a Gushe where the actors repeat a word and transform it into a song. The actor repeats a word without rhythm for the first time and after three or four times, he repeats the same word, adding rhythm to it and setting it to music so that the actors can sing and dance.

Sometimes the servant is wrong to say a word, and practically his boss begins to correct him. However, the servant does not learn or, to put it more accurately, does not want to learn and practically makes fun of him. In the end, the roles switch, and the servant pronounces the words perfectly while the master does not pronounce them well. In another scene, the servant pretends that a small object is very heavy and cannot move it, but the master comes and effortlessly moves it. However, when the master needs to move something very heavy, the servant is able to move it with just one hand.

3. Improvisation

Surely, one of the most important expressive characteristics of Persian comedy techniques was improvisation. This is another analogy to the Commedia dell'Arte.

Siro Ferrone believes that the art of improvisation is rooted in the skill of selecting and coordinating in a timely manner, drawing from individual repertoires and capitalizing on the opportunities presented by the reactions of the audience or the flow of the stage performance. The latter may be outlined in a basic manner through a simple plot (canvas, subjects, scenarios), or more precisely defined through a complete work, from which the actors had already extracted their own parts.[342]

---

[342] Siro Ferrone, *La Commedia dell'Arte. Italian actresses and actors in Europe (16th-18th centuries)*, 93.

In Persia, many actors were illiterate, so if there was a screenplay or written text, they relied on those who could read to help them remember all the actions by heart.

In this spectacular performance, there were various types of actors, and as soon as they joined the acting group, they knew which type they were assigned to play. Each actor had their own acting techniques, which were known to all others. Additionally, there were some shared techniques, known as "Gushes," that all the actors were familiar with. But sometimes the actors would engage in jokes by drawing on silly and amusing memories from their personal lives, seamlessly incorporating them into the performance.

In the show, when the spectators enjoyed a scene, the actors naturally continued in the same manner that the audience desired. Many unexpected events occurred, and if an actor was familiar with the story, they could respond effectively. The actors had to have flexible bodies; in fact, most of them were also skilled dancers. Before the play, the actors rehearsed, training each other in improvisation.

Persian actors did not have special exercises to perfect the art of improvisation. Everything that happened on stage came from their personal experience and knowledge of the performances of other famous actors.

However, when the actors on the stage realized that their performance was pleasing to the spectators, they continued to act in the manner that was particularly appreciated. This also pertained to their criticisms of society and politics, which were either suppressed or encouraged based on the approval expressed by those in attendance.

Sometimes the actors mingled with the audience and performed among them, occasionally posing questions to them as well. Their talent for mimicking the audience's dialects or accents was so impressive that spectators would often become irritated by the actors' antics. The performance was very engaging, and its development was strongly influenced by the audience present.

As for improvisation in the Commedia dell'Arte, Cesare Molinari believes that the actors performed in a manner similar to that of a jazz band.[343] This includes a rhythmic structure in which each instrument intervenes in support or as a soloist, paying attention to the spaces and pauses that open up in the orchestral texture or that respond to thematic suggestions from other instruments' initiatives.

4. The scene and the scenography

In the final years of the Safavid government, as the foundations of the Taghlid show began to take shape, there were no dedicated theatre buildings. Solo actors and buffoons would either perform at the royal court or, occasionally, in the bustling marketplaces where many travelers gathered, or even in coffee shops.[344]

Subsequently, during the Qajar period, it became common to invite comedians to perform in the gardens or courtyards of the aristocrats' houses, in addition to the existing theatrical venues. This was done to entertain and delight the guests.[345]

Usually, the shape of the stage for comedy shows in the Safavid and Qajar periods was semi-circular, with the spectators surrounding the area of the action.

Probably in Persia, the semicircular shape derived from ancient architectural forms. In fact, as we have already seen, during the Qajar period, the Takhte Hozi show took place in gardens or courtyards, where actors performed on small stages set up at the foot of fountains. If an actor was not on

---

343 Cesare Molinari, *History of the theatre*, 107.

344 Bahram Beyzaee, *Theatre in Iran*, [Namāyish dar Īrān], 169.

345 Ibid 171-172.

stage, he would come down and sit in a corner. When the scene was needed, he would go back on stage.[346]

Rarely, some of the actors would surprise the audience by sitting among them and suddenly starting to perform, before eventually taking the stage.

In the final years of the Safavid government, the actors who performed comedic shows did not have access to elaborate stage setups, primarily due to economic limitations. However, this lack precisely determined a characteristic of Persian comedy, which typically did not include elaborate or costly scenography. Actors, especially in the nineteenth century, would typically bring the necessary items on stage in crates, which eventually transformed into authentic stage accessories over time. But the most important aspect in relation to the scenography was the implicit pact between actors and the audience. An empty scene and a subtle gesture from the actor were enough for the spectators to immediately understand, by example, that the scene was taking place in the desert.[347] The actors' evocative capacity was therefore fundamental.

5. Music and singing

Music and singing are among the main elements of Persian comedy. Most of these songs were either famous Iranian folk songs or compositions by actors. The main instruments are the Tar, Tonbak, and Kamancheh, which accompany the dance and singing of the actors, bringing joy and happiness to the audience. Usually, the musicians had a bandstand on the right side at the front of the stage, where they would play a song as the actors entered and exited the stage. In certain locations, the music filled the vacant gaps of the

[346] Yaghub Azhand, *Theatre of the Qajars*, [Namāyish dar dawrah-i Qājār], 278-280.

[347] Bahram, Beyzaee, *Theatre in Iran*, [Namāyish dar Īrān], 168.

performance, providing the actor with time to prepare for their role. In certain instances, music was incorporated into the performance as a technique, allowing various theatrical situations to be conveyed to the audience through music. In Iranian comedy, there were different dances such as the Bell dance, the *Shateri* dance, *Shish kebab* dance, Cherry dance, Yogurt dance, and wooden dance, which were performed in different parts of the play.

6. The travels of Persian Comedy

As Siro Ferrone recalls,[348] the diffusion of Commedia dell'Arte at a European level, starting with countries such as France or Spain, has caused changes in the typology of the characters and in the spectacular form. The influence of French diffusion of the Commedia dell'Arte is particularly significant. As Vito Pandolfi had previously emphasized,[349] it brought about profound changes in both the performances, often centered on mythological parody, and the characters.

In Persia, from the final years of the Safavid government until the conclusion of the Qajar period, Persian comedy embarked on numerous journeys within the country's borders. Additionally, it gradually expanded its reach to neighboring countries such as Azerbaijan, Turkey, and Tajikistan. Comedians, if they did not feel comfortable in one city, would emigrate and continue their work in another country.

After the Afghan attack during the reign of Shah Sultan Husein, all the comic solo actors in Isfahan relocated to other cities to continue their shows. Subsequently, with the establishment of the Afsharid government and the capital

---

[348] Siro Ferrone, *La Commedia dell'Arte. Italian actresses and actors in Europe (16th-18th centuries)*, 3.

[349] Vito Pandolfi, *The Theater of the Renaissance and the Commedia dell'Arte*,(Rome, Lerici, 1969), 215.

being transferred to Mashhad, many artists from the theatre scene also moved there.

Later, after the Afsharids,[350] came the Zand dynasty. The capital of the dynasty was Shiraz, which became an excellent earning opportunity for the most famous artists and actors. In the Zand period, the capital changed several times between Isfahan, Kerman, and Tehran. These changes were systematically followed by the relocation of the acting companies.

These displacements were responsible for the linguistic variety of the actors' performances that we have referred to.

In the period of the Qajar government, when the capital was established in Tehran, there were many comedians who traveled to the capital to present their performances before the king and the princes. They hoped to enter the service of the royal court if their performance was appreciated by the sovereign.

In the magnificent tradition of Taghlid, multiple dialects from different Persian cities were used, reflecting the nomadic nature of the actors. This also allowed for the portrayal of characters connected to specific local contexts. For example, if there was a miserly character in a show, he spoke with the accent of the city of Isfahan. The inhabitants of Isfahan, known for their stinginess due to their engagement in rich commercial activities, were often portrayed in this manner. Or, if he was an easygoing individual, he spoke in the dialect of Shiraz, known for its reputation of having a placid and quiet population.

The migration of comedy focused on the regions along the northern and southern borders of Persia, which were strategically significant due to their proximity to the Caspian Sea and the Persian Gulf. From northern Persia, travelers and

---

[350] They were governors of Persia from 1736 to 1750.

theatre scholars arrived from Russia and other countries, such as Azerbaijan, thus allowing the influence of other theatrical cultures on Persian comedy. This influence can be seen in the works of authors such as Hasan Moghadam and Akhundzadeh. By contrast, in the southern region of the country, due to the significant influence of Portuguese and Spanish individuals who had regular political and commercial connections with Persia, a notable character named Firuz (servant) emerged. It is believed that Firuz originated from the black servants who arrived in Persia as a result of the Portuguese and Spanish presence.

In the final years of the Qajar government, Persian comedy faced significant obstacles and censorship from both the government and certain intellectuals who deemed it a crude form of entertainment. Censorship was also a significant obstacle to the movement of comedians between the different cities of Persia, frequently encountering the hostility of the local governors. At the same time, however, it also contributed to increasing the frequency of company movements.

7. Language

There are two types of languages and dialects in Persian comedy. This is defined according to their social position in society: the lower class and the upper class. The king, the minister, and the nobles belong to the upper class of society and speak in a more formal and pretentious manner. On the other hand, there are also black actors in the show who speak with a different accent. Siah does not pronounce words and names correctly, which causes laughter. Theatre groups mostly traveled to cities and occasionally to neighboring countries around Qajar Iran in order to earn a living. Naturally, each city had its own distinct dialects. Actors also attempted to incorporate the unique vocabulary of the city in order to warmly greet the audience. Of course, these words gradually became part of their theatrical vocabulary, and as a result, a new theatrical language emerged among the actors.

8. A possible occurrence

Looking at the history and civilization of Iran and Italy, one can understand the extent and depth of the different relations between these two countries in different periods of history. Relations that have naturally led to cultural, linguistic and, of course, artistic integrations. In the meantime, theatre has not been exempt from this theme, and it has undoubtedly received some influences in the midst of these movements. It is obvious that Iranian comedy is very similar to its Italian counterpart, but how it came about remains to be studied in depth.

But perhaps one of the most important reasons that caused this impact is the travel of European travelers to Iran and also the travel of Iranians to the West. But a very important document that details the performance of a show under the Tekie Dowlat can strengthen this theory; "Etemad ol-Saltaneh" writes in his newspaper that:

> I heard that yesterday (September 13, 1888) in the 'Tekie of Dowlat' was performed the 'Tazie' of Solomon. There were present English and Italian ambassadors with their followers. After the end of the 'Tazie,' a Persian comedian named Esmail Bazaz entered the stage along with about two hundred other comedians. They all wore white beards and were dressed as Persian, foreign and Italian comedians. They performed a comic scene that could have been vulgar. The scene in 'Tazie' was even

worse than a 'Tamasha khaneh.' After that we left with Amin al Doleh and went home in a carriage.[351]

[۶۷۶] جمعه ۷ – دیروز قرار شد صبح بعد از روضه دربخانه بروم. شنیدم دیشب درتکیهٔ
دولت تعزیهٔ دیرسلیمان بوده و سفرای انگلیس و ایطالیا با اتباعشان آمده بودند تماشا. بعد از
ختم تعزیه اسماعیل بزاز مقلد معروف با قریب دویست نفر از مقلدین و عملهٔ طرب بودند که با
ریشهای سفید و عاریه و لباسهای مختلف از فرنگی [و] روس و ایرانی ورود به‌تکیه کردند و
حرکات قبیح از خودشان بیرون آوردند. طوری که مجلس تعزیه ازتماشاخانه بدتر شده. به‌اتفاق
امین‌الدوله کالسکه نشسته خانه آمدم.

Fig. 66. Collaboration between Persian and European (Italian) actors, Shah Abdol Azim Harem Library and Archive, Qajar period.

From this document we can understand several things:

1. Foreign spectators who travelled through Persia during the reign of Naser al-Din Shah came to see Tazieh.

2. It was observed that every kind of Persian performance had a certain space for interpretation.
3. The actors either knew or collaborated with European costume designers and Italian actors.

4. Comedy did not hold a high status in Qajar society, particularly among the nobility and religious individuals.

It is very likely that during this period in Persia there were Italian and French actors who performed the art of comedy in different places. Siro Ferrone believes that around 1850 there were Neapolitan comedians who traveled to Asia to give performances. Ferrone's hypothesis confirms that in the 1860s, collaboration between Persian, Italian, and possibly French comedians was still ongoing.

With the beginning of the Industrial Revolution in France, commedia dell'arte came to an end in Europe, and many of its actors immigrated to other countries.

---

[351] Mohamad Hasan Khan Etemad ol saltaneh, *Ruznameye khaterat*, 591.

As mentioned above, Persia and Italy maintained very close relations in different periods of history, and economic, political and religious relations have also led to cultural influences. Of course, dramatic effects do not emerge overnight and it takes a lot of time, but as I said, the different relations between these two cultures emerged in different historical periods and bore another fruit, that of theatrical culture, which can be clearly seen in different arts. But the result of these fusions in Commedia dell' arte and Takhte Hozi is very stimulating and worth exploring.

Considering the settlement of nationals of different countries in Iran during the Qajar period as well as the presence of consulates of different countries, each of these countries brought musicians and artists to Iran in addition to their family members. There is the Dar al-Funun auditorium, which was built in the Dar al-Funun school with a French design in 1877 under the supervision of Ali Akbar Khan Mazaian al Dole and could boast a capacity of 300 spectators.[352]

The first Persian performers who appeared in this theater building had no knowledge of European theatre; therefore, they depended on instruction from European artists who went to Persia. These artists were usually selected among those who came to Iran from Europe to teach at the Dar al-Funun school.[353]

Hassan Shirvani (1895-1951 Tehran) recalls that "Mozaian al Dole, in collaboration with other famous comedy actors such as Karim Shiree and Esmail Bazaz, created plays such as

---

352 Niyayesh, Pur Hassan, *the theater in Iran (Dar ol Fonun)*, Jaryān-i ̣talīʻah-'i tiyātr dar Īrān va sarguzasht-i tamāshākhānah-'i Dār al-Funūn (Tehran, Kule poshti 2017), 122.

353 Mostafa Oskuee, *History of Iranian Theater*,[Sayrī dar tārīkh-i ti'ātr-i Īrān], 161.

Molière's *Forced Marriage*. The actors did not act according to the script but tried to improvise by knowing the text."[354]

The arrival of European artists in Iran and of famous plays, which were mostly comedies, opened the way for collaboration between Iranian and European actors, especially French and Italian. Undoubtedly, Molière was one of the first and most important European writers whose plays came to Iran. Molière and his unique comedies were not performed in the same French way in Iran, but the translators of these works tried to align these plays with the culture and aspirations of Iranian society.

Persian comedy and commedia dell'arte were both born at the same time and from the hearts of society and the people. Both traveled around and absorbed many influences to find their final form. With the beginning of the French Revolution, the commedia dell'arte slowly approached its demise. In the last years of the Qajar government, Persian comedy was strongly hampered and censored by the government and some intellectuals, who considered it a very vulgar type of play. The censorship was also a considerable obstacle to the movement of comedians between the various cities of Persia, which often met with the hostility of the local governors. At the same time, however, it also contributed to making the movements of the companies more frequent. As we noted, from the beginning of the Safavid period, many travelers from Europe, including the Republic of Venice, came to Iran, and in their diaries, they had detailed descriptions of Iranian shows. During the Qajar period, Iranian political leaders' trips to Europe made Iranians familiar with European shows. These trips between Iran and Europe certainly created dramatic effects. In view of the above points, we have learned about the similarities and closeness of Persian comedy and the commedia dell'arte.

---

[354] Hassan Shirvani, *Artistic Activities in 50 Years of the Pahlavi Empire*, (Tehran, Vezarat Farhang va Honar, 1971), 27.

Undoubtedly, both cultures have strong theatrical abilities, and the different relations between these two cultures created a theatrical proximity, and of course, both could indirectly influence each other, but this does not mean that either of these two forms of performance changed the cause of their creation.

AFTERWORD

Theater during the Qajar period can be considered one of the most tumultuous periods in the entire history of Iranian theatre. A period that was the heir of Safavid religious shows on the one hand and witnessed the mainstreaming of Iranian comedy on the other hand. But more importantly, the entry of foreign theatre into Iran, much like many other events imported from Farang, occurred without creating an appropriate platform for the people. Willingly or unwillingly, the strangers' theatre entered Iran and gradually established itself in theatres across various cities.

European theatre had made its way into Iran, and ironically, some government officials had welcomed it. However, the main question remained: did Iranian plays have the capacity to evolve and adapt?

Etemad ol-Sataneh writes in his diary:[355]

> After lunch, Naser al din Shah asked us to enter the garden. Karim Shirei and his actors made Taghlids and wrestled, including the Austrian style... I said to the king: despite the high cost of travel in Europe, our actors are now imitating the Austrian style. This is a good thing, I said sarcastically … and the king laughed… although he didn't like it....

Undoubtedly, the exchange and positive influence of one society on another can contribute to the progress of a nation. However, blindly rejecting one's own cultural heritage and embracing another culture without considering its

---

[355] Mohamad Hasan Khan Etemad ol saltaneh, *Journal of Memories*, [Khạ̄tirāt-i I'timād al-Saḷtanah], 10 April 1882.

compatibility with the society's values can lead to decline and cultural disintegration within that country.

Centuries ago, when strangers came to Iran, they observed, documented, gathered, and brought back various items under different pretexts, such as establishing familiarity, providing assistance, and facilitating communication with Europe. Perhaps due to their political and military superiority, they wanted to showcase their culture and art. The most interesting thing is that, later on, they exported the same achievements of art and culture from the East to us, but under different titles.

But what happened in Iran?

From the Safavid era to the end of the Qajar period, we witness what might be called the most amazing period in Iran's drama, a time when Iranian theatre embarked on the winding path it has traveled on up to the present day. Theatre made its way with difficulty. Despite the bans on ta'ziyah and comedy, the latter continued unabated.

During the Qajar period, there were two classes of people who harmed the culture and art of this land as much as they could from the very beginning, men in politics with a sword that should have been used to fight Iran's enemies but that began to cut down its own ancient cultural tree into pieces, trying instead to cultivate the surface of Western pleasure.

On the other hand, there were religious individuals who viewed art and culture as contrary to their own interests. They attempted to impede the progress of art and culture by excessively emphasizing and promoting their personal religious beliefs and opinions. But the roots of this ancient tree were so deeply rooted in the ground that it did not dry up.

In any case, there were many exchanges between Iran and Europe, and the theatre also benefited from such interactions.

The knowledge of European theatre was incorporated into it, and naturally, it had an impact on its western counterparts. If our efforts were comparable to those of western researchers in the field of translation and the dissemination of dramatic culture, maybe today we would have witnessed other events with respect to the world's knowledge of Iranian theatre.

Bibliography

Abd allah Mostofi, *Explaining of My life*, Sharḥ-i zindagānī-i man, yā, Tārīkh-i ijtimāʻī va idārī-i dawrah-i Qājārīyah , (Tehran, Zavar, 1998).

Abolghasem Janati Ataee, *Iranian Theatre*, [Bunyād-i namāyish dar Īrān], (Tehran ,Safi Al Shah, 1977).

Abu Rayhan Muhammad ibn Ahmad al-*Biruni, Al Tafhim,* (Tehran Majles, 1937).

Abu Rayhan Muhammad ibn Ahmad al-Biruni, translated by Akbar, Danaseresht, *Asar ol bagieh*,(Tehran Amir Kabir, 1984).

Abubakr Narshakhi, *The history of Bukhara*, Tus, Tehran 2008.

Aleksandro Chodzko, translator Jalal Satari, The Iranian Theater, (Tehran Faslnameye Theatre), 1990.

Aleksandro Chodzko, translator Jalal Satari, *The Persian theater*, (Teheran, Faslnameye theatre, 1990).

Alexandre Dumas, translator Mohamad Taher Mirza Eskandari, *Louis XIV et son siècle*,(Tehran, Danesh mozafari, 1904).

Ali Akbar Dehkhoda, *Dehkhoda Dictionary*, Lughatnāmah-'i Fārsī Banke ,(Tehran Melli, 1940).

Amir Alizadegan, *History of the Theater of Tabriz*, (Tehran Faslnameye teatr, 1988.

Arakel Davrizhetsi, edited by L.A. Khanlarian, *Story of Arakel*, (Iravan, Academy of Science of Armenia and Russia, 1990).

Azod ol doleh, History of Azodi, [Tārīkh-i ʻAẕudī], (Tehran, Abdol Hoseyn Navaee, 1977).

Bahram Beyzaee, *Theatre in Iran*, [Namāyish dar Īrān], Roshangaran, Tehran 1964.

Basil Nikitin, translator Ali Frah vashi, *The Iran I Know*, (Tehran Marefat, 1977).

Carla Serena, translator Golamreza Samee, *Iran's people and sights*, Mardum va dīdanīhā-yi Īrān : safar′nāmah,(Tehran, Nashre No, 1984).

Carsten Neibuhr, traduttore Parviz Rajabi, *Carsten Neibuhr's travelogue*,[Safarnāmah-'i Kārstin Nībūr], (Tehran, Tuka, 1975).

Cesare Molinari, *La Commedia dell'Arte*, (Milan, Mondadori, 1985).

Charles Felix Texier, *Description de l'Arménie, la Perse et la Mésopotamie,* (Paris F. Didot frères, 1852).

Corneille Le Brun, *Voyages de Corneille Le Brun Per la Moscovie en Perse*, (Amsterdam, Freres Wetstein, 1718).

Count de Sercey, translator Ehsan Eshraghi, *Persia in 1839-1840*, (Tehran, SoKhan, 2010).

Edmond O'Donvan, *Today's Iran*, (London, Oasis, 1882).

Enayat Allah Shahidi, Research in *Ta'ziyah h and Ta'ziyah h Khani*, [Pizhūhishī dar taʻzīyah va taʻzīyah′khvānī : az āghāz tā pāyān-i dawrah-'i Qājār dar Tihrān], (Daftar-i Pizhūhish′hā-yi Farhangī : Kumīsiyūn- i Millī-i Yūniskū dar Īrān, 2002).

Eugene Aubin, translator Ali Asgar Saidi, *Today's Iran*, (Tehran, Zavar, 1983).

Fereidun Adamiat, *Amir kabir and Iran*, [Amīr Kabīr va Īrān], (Tehran, Kharazmi, 1977).

Gaspar Drouvolle, translator Manuchehr Etemad Moghadam, *Voyage en Perse, atlas*, (Tehran, shabaviz, 1986).

Giacomo, Oreglia, *La Commedia dell'Arte,* translator Natalie Choobineh, (Tehran Ghatreh, 2002).

Gilbert Moshk Anbarians, *A look at Armenian theater in Iran*, (Tehran, Faslnameye Peyman, 2005,).

Hanry D'Allemagne, translator Homayun, *the travel memory from Khorasan to Bakhtiari*, (Tehran, Frahvashi, 1999).

Haroton Drhohanian, translator Leon Minasian, *History of Jolfa of Isfahan*, [Tārīkh-i Julfā-yi Iṣfahān](Isfahan Zende Rud, 2000).

Hasan Amid, *Amid vocabulary*, Farhang-i 'Amīd (Fārsī), (Tehran, Amir kabir, 1983).

Hashem Razi, *The calendar of ancient Persia*, Pizhūhishī dar gāhshumārī va jashn'hā-yi Īrān-i bāstān(Tehran Farvehar, 1979).

Hassan Shirvani, *Artistic Activities in 50 Years of the Pahlavi Empire*, (Tehran, Vezarat Farhang va Honar, 1971).

Herbert Morris, *Mohammad Reza Beyk Persian Ambassador in the court of Louis XIV*, Abdol Hoseyn Vojdani, (Tehran, Gozaresh 1 983).

Hoseyn ibn Mohamad ibn Tahvildar Isfahan, *The geography of Isfahan*, [Jughrāfiyā-yi Iṣfahān : jughrāfiyā-yi ṭabīʻī va insānī va āmār-i aṣnāf-i shahr], (Tehran, Akhtaran, 2009).

It is from a manuscript by Mirza Agha Tabrizi, *Four plays and Ehical book*, [Chahār tiyātr], (Tabriz, Ibn Sina, 1976).

J.B Fraser, translator Manuchehr Amiri, *Winter travel memoirs*, (Tehran, Tus, 1984).

Jafar Shahri, *Social history of Teherean in the 13th century*, [Tārīkh-i ijtimāʻī-i Tihrān dar qarn-i sīzdahum : zindagī, kasb va kār], (Tehran, Yasa va Esmailian, 1389).

Jakob Eduard Polak, translator Keikavus Jahandari, *Iran and Iranian*,[Safarnāmah-i Pūlāk : Irān va Irāniyān], (Tehranm, Kharazmi, 1989).

Jakob Eduard Polak, translator Keikavus Jahandari, *Iran and Iranian*, [Safarnāmah-i Pūlāk : Irān va Irāniyān] (Tehran, Kharazmi, 1983).

James Morier, translator Abolghasem Seri, *Travel memoirs*, (Tehran, Tus, 2007).

Jamshid Malek pur, *Persian dramatic literature*, [Adabīyāt-i namāyishī dar Īrān], (Tehran, Tus, 1983).

Jean-Baptiste Tavernier, translator Hamid Arbab Shiran, *Les Six voyages*,(Tehran Nilufar, 2002).

John M. Marincola, *the Histories*, (London, Penguiin, 1959).

John Malcolm, translator Mirza Ismail Heyrat, *History of Persia*, Afsun 1990.

Mania Ghazarian, translator Edik Baghdasarian, *The paintings of new Jolfa of Isfahan*, Hovik (Tehran, Ogharian, 1984).

Martin Vermazern, *Mithraism*, translated by Bozorg Naderzad, (Tehran, Cheshmeh, 2001).

Mary Boyce, translator Mehri Sharafi, *The Parthian Gosans in Iran*, (Tehran Chista, 1990).

Mayel Baktash, *Evolution of Taghlid*, (Tehran, Faslnameye Teatr, 1984).

Mehdi Malekzade, *History of the Iranian Constitutional Revolution*, [Tārīkh-i inqilāb-i mashrụ̄tīyat-i Īrān], (Tehran, Sokhan 2004).

Mohamad Ali Katuzian Tehrani, *Analysis and Research on the Persian Constitutional Revolution*, [Mushāhidāt va taḥlīl-i ijtimāʿī va siyāsī az tārīkh-i inqilāb-i mashrụ̄tīyat-i Īrān Enteshar], (Tehran, Intishar, 2000).

Mohamad Hasan Khan Etemad ol saltaneh, *Al-Moaser Al-Asar, in forty years of Iranian history*, (Tehran Asatir, 1984).

Mohamad Hasan Khan Etemad ol saltaneh, *Journal of Memories*, [Khạ̄tirāt-i Iʿtimād al-Saḷtanah], (Tehran, Amir kabir, 1893).

Mohamad Karim Pir nia, *the form of the architecture of Iran*, Tehran, Islamic Art, 2002).

Mohamad Reza Zamani Zavarzadeh, *Theatre in Mash had*, (Tehran Faslnameye teatr, 1988).

Mohammad Ali Jamalzadeh, *Folk vocabulary*, [Farhang-i lughāt-i ʿāmiyānah], (Tehran, Abu Sina, 1862).

Mohammad amin Kalateh, *The oldest religious mourning*, «Newspaper of Tehran emruz».

Mohammad Hasan khan Etemad ol Saltaneh, edited by Iraj Afshar *The Diary of Etemad ol Saltaneh*, [Rūznāmah-'i khāṭirāt-i I'timād al-Salṭanah], Amir Kabir, Tehran, 1966).

Morteza Ahmadi, *Kohne haye hamishe no*, [Kuhnahā-i hamīšā nau : tarānahā-i taḫt-i ḥauḍī ; wīrāst-i duwwum], (Tehran, Quqnūs,2001).

Mostafa Oskuee, *History of Iranian Theater*,[Pizhūhishī dar tārīkh-i ti'ātr-i Īran], (Tehran, Anahita, 1992).

Mria Francesca Tiepolo, *La ripubblica di Venezia*, transleated by Iraj Anvar, (Tehran, Bahman, 1973).

Naser al din Shah Qajar, edited by Fatemeh Ghazi ha, *Diary of Naser al-Din Shah,* [Rūznāmah-'i khāṭirāt-i Nāṣir al-Dīn Shāh], (Tehran, Research Office of the National Documents Organization of Iran , 1993).

Naser al din shah, Edited by Majid Abd Amin, *Diary of Naser al-Din Shah Qajar the first trip in Europe*, [Rūznāmah-'i khāṭirāt-i Nāṣir al-Dīn Shāh Qājār : az Shavvāl-i 1288 tā Ẕīḥijjah-i 1290], (Tehran, Dr, Mahmud Afshar, 2020).

Nazim-al-Islam Kermani, History *of Iranian Awakening*, [Tārīkh-i bīdārī-i Īrāniyān] Volume 1, Saeedi Sirjani's effort, (Farhang Foundation, Tehran 1967)

Nezami, *Haft Peykar*, Ebn sina, Tehran 1955.

Niyayesh Pur Hassan, *(Dar ol Fonun)*, [Jaryān-i ̣talīʻah-'i tiyātr dar Īrān va sarguẕasht-i tamāshākhānah-'i Dār al-Funūn], (Tehran, Kule poshti 2017).

Niyayesh Pur hassan, *Iranians' recognition movement with Moliere*, (Tehran, Kuleh Poshti, 2019).

Niyayesh, Pur Hassan, *the theater in Iran (Dar ol Fonun)*, Jaryān-I ̣talīʻah-'i tiyātr dar Īrān va sarguẕasht-i tamāshākhānah-'i Dār al-Funūn (Tehran, Kule poshti 2017).

Robert B. M. Binning, *A Journal of Two Years' Travel in Persia*, 2 vols,(London, Ceylon, 1857).

Ruh ollah Khaleghi, *History of Persian Music*, [Sarguẕasht-i mūsīqī-i Īrān], (Tehran Safi ali Shah, 1975).

Siro Ferrone, *La Commedia dell'Arte. Italian actresses and actors in Europe (16th-18th centuries)*, (Torino Einaudi, 2014).

Vito Pandolfi, *The Theater of the Renaissance and the Commedia dell'Arte*,(Rome, Lerici, 1969).

William Bayne Fisher, translator Yaghub Azhand, *History of the Safavids*, (Tehran Jami, 1949).

Yaghub Azhand, *theatre of the Safavids*, [Namāyish dar dawrah-'i Ṣafavī], Asare Honari, Tehran 2009.

Yahya Zoka and Mohamad Hasan Semsar, *Tehran in pictures*, [Tihrān dar taṣvīr], (Tehran, Sorosh, 1980).

Yahya Zoka, *History of Golestan Castle*,[Tārīkhchah-i sākhtimānhā-yi Arg-i Saḷtanatī-i Tihrān : va rāhnamā-yi Kākh-i Gulistān], (Tehran Anjoman asar Meli, 1970).

Archives and Libraries

Organization of Astan Quds Razavi Libraries, Museums and Documentation Center, Mashhad, Iran.

Golestan Palace World Heritage Collection, Tehran, Iran.

Borujerd cultural heritage department, Borujerd, Iran.

Haram Shah Abdol Azim Library, Rey, Iran.

Ministry of Foreign Affairs document archive, Tehran, Iran.

Vank Church Museum, Isfahan, Iran.

Archivio Storico La Stampa Torin, Italia.

Archive of Foreign Policy of the Russian Empire (AVPRI), (Архив внешней политики Российской империи), Mosco, Russia.

The National Archives of Hungary, Budapest, Hungary.

National library of Paris (Bibliothèque nationale de France), Paris, French.

Archives of the Royal Palace - State Archives of Belgium, Brussels, Belgium.

Political archive and historical service (Politisches Archiv und Historischer Dienst), Berlin, Germany.

Austrian State Archives – Vienna, Austria.

Royal Library of Paris

About the Author:

A former Postdoctoral Fellow with the Elahé Omidyar Mir-Djalali Institute of Iranian Studies, Duman Riyazi 's research interests include artefacts and manuscript documents of the *commedia dell'arte*, the theatrical relationship between East and West, the history of Persian theatre and Persian comedy. He has written numerous articles on *la commedia dell'arte* and the modernization of Persian theatre. His publications also include translations of several plays by Carlo Goldoni and *commedia dell'arte* plays by Siro Ferrone. Since 2012, he has initiated numerous conferences and workshops on the inspiration Western theatre has derived from Middle Eastern theatrical forms, especially those of Persian theatre. It is worth mentioning that during his studies in Italy (2013-2020), he collaborated with Professor Siro Ferrone, one of the world's leading academic experts in the field of the *commedia dell' arte*. This collaboration was very valuable for his development in the area of facilitating dialogue among communities. During this time he was frequently invited to give intercultural workshops at various universities. Most of these workshops focused on the artistic relations between Iran and the West from 1501 to 1930.

Asemana Books

Devoted to Publishing Diasporic, Underrepresented and Progressive Literature on the Middle East.

Email: Asemanabooks@gmail.com

Webpage: asemanabooks.ca

Scholarly and Academic Research

- *Solar Calender and the Endurance of Nowruz in Persian Time Culture* – Abbas Amanat – 2025
- *Theatre in Travel* – Duman Riyazi – 2025
- *Tanglusha of a Thousand Images: Essays on Culture and Literature* – Reza Farokhfal – 2024
- *Language, People, and Society: Iranian Minority Languages and Literary Traditions* – Edited by Amir Kalan, Mahdi Ganjavi, Anisa Jafari, Lale Javanshir – 2024
- *Music on the Borderland: Remembering and Chronicling the 1979 Revolution's Shadow on Iranian Music* – Keyan Emami – 2024
- *Implications of Class Analysis in Capitalist Imperialism* – Mohammad Hajinia and Shahrzad Mojab – 2024
- *Dark Night and Phoenixes of the Ashes: Nima Yushij's Poetry from 1932–1942* – Ramin Ahmadi – 2024
- *Whispers of Oasis: Likoo's Poetic Mirage* – Mahdi Ganjavi, Amin Fatemi, Mansour Alimoradi – 2024
- *Hafez and Irony* – Reza Farokhfal – 2024

- *Kurdish Women at the Core of the Historical Contradictions on Feminism and Nationalism* – Shahrzad Mojab – 2023
- *The Peasant Uprising of Mukriyan 1952–1953: Consulate Documents, Diplomatic Correspondence, and the Press Coverage* – Amir Hassanpour – 2022

Critical Edition

- *Rayhan-e Bustan-afruz* – Mirza Agha Khan Kermani, edited by M. Rezaei Tazik – 2025
- *Takwin wa Tashri'* – Mirza Agha Khan Kermani, edited by M. Rezaei Tazik – 2025
- *The Art of Speaking and Writing* – Mirza Agha Khan Kermani, edited by M. Rezaei Tazik – 2025
- *The History of Changes in Iran* – Mirza Agha Khan Kermani, edited by M. Rezaei Tazik – 2024
- *Rostam in the Twenty-Second Century* – Abdulhussain San'atizadeh Kermani, edited by Mahdi Ganjavi and M. Mansouri – 2017

Poetry

- *Shape of Extinction* – Poetry of Bijan Jalali, Translated by Adeeba Shahid Talukder and Aria Fani - 2025
- *One Hundred Nights of Yearning* – Mansour Noorbakhsh – 2025
- *Songs of Barbad* – Amir Hakimi – 2024
- *With My Shadows, I Created Myself* – Hadi Ebrahimi Roudbaraki - 2024

- *Citizens of September* – Saeid Rezadoust - 2024
- *Wonder of Memory* – Amir Hakimi – 2023
- *Galaxy Has No Memory of the Sunset* – Mahdi Ganjavi – 2023
- *Strangers Who Live in Me* – Mahdi Ganjavi – 2021
- *Exiled to the Rocky* – Ali Fatolahi – 2018

Fiction & Plays

- *Bari* – Behrooz Bedakhshan – 2025
- *Escape from the Girl's Complex* – Mahbobe Mousavi – 2025
- *Yousef, Joseph, Guiseppe* – Ali Foumani - 2025
- *An Iranian Odyssey* – Rana Soleimani – 2025
- *Lead to Evil* – Javad Alavi – 2025
- *We Are Drunk and Broken, and No One Is Witnessing Us* – Mahdi Ganjavi – 2025
- *Someone Had Died in Front of Our House* – Akbar Falahzadeh – 2024
- *Zinat* – Vahid Zarrabi Nasab – 2024
- *Siberian Crane* – Ali Foumani - 2024
- *Elephants Reached the Plain* – Kaveh Oveisi - 2024
- *Textual Mosaic* – Marzieh Sotoudeh – 2024
- *Expectations of a Dream* – Mahdi Ganjavi – 2020

Asemana Books is devoted to publishing diasporic, underrepresented, and progressive literature on the Middle East.

asemanabooks.ca

ASEMANA
BOOKS

www.ingramcontent.com/pod-product-compliance
Lightning Source LLC
LaVergne TN
LVHW010650110826
845149LV00014B/3013
* 9 7 8 1 9 9 7 5 0 3 3 5 4 *